1
uno

¡Avancemos!

LECTURAS para TODOS
with TEST PREPARATION

HOLT McDOUGAL
a division of Houghton Mifflin Harcourt

Acknowledgements

"Cumpleaños," from *Family Pictures/Cuadros de familia* by Carmen Lomas Garza. Copyright © 1990 by Carmen Lomas Garza. All rights reserved. Reprinted with the permission of the publisher, Children's Book Press, San Francisco, CA.

"La exclamación" and "En Uxmal" by Octavio Paz. © Octavio Paz, 1970. Reprinted by permission.

"Palma sola" by Nicolás Guillén. © Herederos de Nicolás Guillén. Reprinted by permission of Herederos de Nicolás Guillén c/o Agencia Literaria Latinoamericana.

Excerpt from *Como agua para chocolate* by Laura Esquivel. Copyright © 1989 by Laura Esquivel. Used by permission of Doubleday, a division of Random House, Inc.

"Oda al tomate," from *Odas elementales* by Pablo Neruda. Copyright © Fundación Pablo Neruda, 1954. Reprinted with the permission of Agencia Literaria Carmen Balcells, S.A., Barcelona, Spain.

Illustration and **Photography Credits** appear on page 204.

ISBN-13: 978-0-618-76603-1
ISBN-10: 0-618-76603-0
Internet: www.holtmcdougal.com

10 11 12 13 14   0982   15 14 13 12
4500367179

Contents

Literatura adicional

Academic and Informational Reading

Test Preparation Strategies

Welcome to *Lecturas para todos*

Reading Skills Improvement– in Spanish *and* English

You will read selections from your Spanish textbook as well as readings from great Spanish-language literature. Materials in English will help you practice understanding the types of texts you encounter in school, on tests, and in the real world. As you work with all the selections, you will find your reading skills in both languages improving!

At the end of the book, you will also study and practice strategies for taking standardized tests.

Lecturas culturales and *Literatura adicional*

These readings from your textbook and from Spanish-language literature will give you a chance to improve your reading skills and Spanish vocabulary. You will also gain invaluable cultural insights and have the opportunity to experience great literature.

Before You Read

Before each reading, the *Para leer* page prepares you with features to help you anticipate the content of the reading.

Reading Strategy The strategy and graphic organizer allow you to decide how you will approach the material and to jot down your thoughts.

What You Need to Know This section tells you what to expect before you begin reading and gives you extra insights to help you get the most out of each selection.

While You Read

Point-of-use features next to the selections help you get the most out of each reading and make it your own.

Reading Tip For each selection, you will find a handy, specific reading tip to help with difficult or specialized language.

Lecturas para todos is a hands-on reading text that lets you take notes, highlight, underline text, and organize your thoughts on paper, so that you can master each reading and make it your own. The unique features of *Lecturas para todos* will help you quickly become comfortable with reading in Spanish and sharpen your comprehension skills in both Spanish and English.

Links to ¡Avancemos!

When using McDougal Littell's *¡Avancemos!,* you will find *Lecturas para todos* to be a perfect companion. *Lecturas para todos* lets you mark up the *Lectura cultural* selections as you read, helping you understand and remember more.

Read on to learn more!

A pensar... These critical-thinking questions will help you analyze content as you read.

Márcalo This hands-on feature invites you to mark up the text by underlining and circling words and phrases right on the page.

Gramática Highlighting key grammar concepts will help you reinforce and internalize them.

Vocabulario Marking new vocabulary words in the text lets you practice them and see how they are used in natural contexts.

Análisis This feature appears in the *Literatura adicional* section and encourages you to focus on one aspect of literary analysis as you read.

Reader's Success Strategy These notes give useful and fun tips and strategies for comprehending the selection.

Challenge These activities keep you challenged, even after you have grasped the basic concepts of the reading.

Vocabulary Support

Palabras clave Words that are important to understanding the readings appear in bold. The definitions appear at the bottom of each page.

After You Read

After you have read each selection, you will have the opportunity to practice key vocabulary, check your comprehension, and relate the reading to your own interests and experiences.

Vocabulario de la lectura A list of the *palabras clave* and their definitions is followed by two activities to help you practice these important words.

¿Comprendiste? Questions after each selection check your understanding of what you have read.

Conexión personal These short writing activities ask you to relate the selection to your life and experiences, making what you have read more meaningful to you.

Academic and Informational Reading

Here is a special collection of real-world examples—in English—to help you read every kind of informational material, from textbooks to technical directions. Why are these sections in English? Because the strategies you learn will help you on tests, in other classes, and in the world outside of school. You will find strategies for the following:

Analyzing Text Features This section will help you read many different types of magazine articles and textbooks. You will learn how titles, subtitles, lists, graphics, many different kinds of visuals, and other special features work in magazines and textbooks. After studying this section you will be ready to read even the most complex material.

Understanding Visuals Tables, charts, graphs, maps, and diagrams all require special reading skills. As you learn the common elements of various visual texts, you will learn to read these materials with accuracy and skill.

Recognizing Text Structures Informational texts can be organized in many different ways. In this section you will study the following structures and learn about special key words that will help you identify the organizational patterns:
• Main Idea and Supporting Details
• Problem and Solution
• Sequence
• Cause and Effect
• Comparison and Contrast
• Persuasion

Reading in the Content Areas You will learn special strategies for reading social studies, science, and mathematics texts.

Reading Beyond the Classroom In this section you will encounter applications, schedules, technical directions, product information, Web pages, and other readings. Learning to analyze these texts will help you in your everyday life and on some standardized tests.

Test Preparation Strategies

In this section, you will find strategies and practice to help you succeed on many different kinds of standardized tests. After closely studying a variety of test formats through annotated examples, you will have an opportunity to practice each format on your own. Additional support will help you think through your answers. You will find strategies for the following:

Successful Test Taking This section provides many suggestions for preparing for and taking tests. The information ranges from analyzing test questions to tips for answering multiple-choice and open-ended test questions.

Reading Tests: Long Selections You will learn how to analyze the structure of a lengthy reading and prepare to answer the comprehension questions that follow it.

Reading Tests: Short Selections These selections may be a few paragraphs of text, a poem, a chart or graph, or some other item. You will practice the special range of comprehension skills required for these pieces.

Functional Reading Tests These real-world texts present special challenges. You will learn about the various test formats that use applications, product labels, technical directions, Web pages, and more.

Revising-and-Editing Tests These materials test your understanding of English grammar and usage. You may encounter capitalization and punctuation questions. Sometimes the focus is on usage questions such as verb tenses or pronoun agreement issues. You will become familiar with these formats through the guided practice in this section.

Writing Tests Writing prompts and sample student essays will help you understand how to analyze a prompt and what elements make a successful written response. Scoring rubrics and a prompt for practice will prepare you for the writing tests you will take.

Lecturas culturales

Point-of-use comprehension support helps you read selections from *¡Avancemos!* and develop critical-thinking skills.

Para leer   *Saludos desde San Antonio y Miami*

Reading Strategy

MAKE A COMPARISON CHART Use the chart to compare San Antonio and Miami.

	San Antonio	Miami
Sitios de interés		
Actividades		
Comida		

What You Need to Know

When you think of Spanish-speaking people or cultures, you may imagine Spain or Mexico. However, did you know that Spanish is the second most widely spoken language in the United States? You don't have to travel far to find elements of Spanish-speaking culture or to hear people conversing in Spanish. In the following reading, you will learn about two U.S. cities where you would likely meet many Spanish speakers.

Unidad 1, Lección 2
Saludos desde San Antonio y Miami   7

Reading Strategy
Reading tips and strategies give you a game plan for approaching the material and making sense of what you read.

What You Need to Know
Additional information and background provide you with a key to unlock the selection so that you can better understand and enjoy it.

Lecturas culturales   *continued*

Reading Tip
Help with difficult or specialized language lowers the barriers to comprehension.

Reader's Success Strategy
These strategies offer suggestions to help you read the selection successfully. Sometimes you will have a chart to fill in while you read; other times you will find ideas for mentally organizing the information you find.

READING TIP As you learn Spanish, you will be able to recognize many Spanish words that look and sound like English words. These words are called cognates. Make a list of all of the cognates you can find in the reading and what they mean in English.

READER'S SUCCESS STRATEGY As you read, compare the descriptions of each city with the photos you see. What elements of each city's description are pictured?

Saludos desde San Antonio y Miami

En San Antonio, Texas, **hay** parques de diversiones, museos y están el Paseo del Río y el Álamo. Después de las clases, a los chicos y a las chicas les gusta pasar un rato con
5 los amigos en El Mercado, donde es posible escuchar música de los mariachis y comer **comida** típica mexicana.

El Álamo en San Antonio, Texas

PALABRAS CLAVE
hay *there is, there are*   **la comida** *food*

8   Lecturas para todos

Level 1

Andar en patineta en Miami, Florida

5

En Miami, Florida, si hace buen tiempo, a
los chicos y a las chicas les gusta andar en
10 patineta o montar en bicicleta. Después de las
clases, a muchos chicos les gusta pasear con
los amigos por la **Calle** Ocho, en la Pequeña
Habana de Miami. ¡Es una pequeña Cuba en
la Florida! Allí es posible comer sándwiches
15 cubanos y beber jugo de mango.

PALABRAS CLAVE
la calle   *street*

⫿ **MÁRCALO** ⊳ **GRAMÁTICA**
You can recognize verbs in
Spanish because they end **-ar,
-er,** or **-ir.** These verbs are in
the infinitive form. They are the
equivalent of "to do…" in English.
For example, **comer** means "to
eat." In the boxed text, underline
all the verbs in the infinitive.

A pensar…

How are the two cities
described in the article
similar to or different from
the area where you live?
(Compare and Contrast)

CHALLENGE Do you think it
would be more interesting to visit
San Antonio or to visit Miami?
Make a list of the features that you
find most attractive in the city of
your choice. **(Evaluate)**

⫿ **MÁRCALO** ⊳ **Gramática**
This feature
assists you with the new
grammar as you read the
selection. Underlining or
circling the examples helps you
internalize and remember the
grammar.

A pensar…
Point-of-use questions check
your understanding and ask
you to think critically about the
passage.

Challenge
This feature asks you to expand
upon what you have learned
from the reading and think
more deeply about the themes
and ideas it contains.

Palabras clave
Important vocabulary words
appear in bold within the
reading. Definitions are given
at the bottom of the page.

Lecturas culturales *continued*

Vocabulario de la lectura
Vocabulary practice follows
each reading, reinforcing the
palabras clave that appear
throughout the selection.
Words that appear in blue are
lesson vocabulary words in
¡Avancemos!

Vocabulario de la lectura

Palabras clave

el (la) amigo(a) *friend*	la comida *food*
la calle *street*	hay *there is, there are*
la chica *girl*	pequeño(a) *little*
el chico *boy*	

A. Match each **Palabra clave** with the word or words to which it is most closely related.

_____ 1. calle   a. personas jóvenes

_____ 2. comida   b. no grande

_____ 3. chicos   c. sándwiches y pizza

_____ 4. amigos   d. pasear y montar en bicicleta

_____ 5. pequeño   e. personas con quienes te gusta pasar un rato

B. Complete each sentence with the correct form of a **Palabra clave.**

1. A los chicos de San Antonio les gusta pasar un rato con

   los _____.

2. En Texas _____ una fortaleza *(fortress)*: el Álamo.

3. Una actividad en Miami es pasear por la _____ Ocho.

4. A los _____ y a las _____ les gusta
   montar en bicicleta.

5. Hay _____ en la Pequeña Habana: sándwiches cubanos.

¿Comprendiste?

1. ¿Qué hay en San Antonio?

_____

2. ¿Qué les gusta hacer después de las clases a los chicos y a las chicas de San Antonio?

_____

3. Si hace buen tiempo en Miami, ¿qué les gusta hacer a los chicos y a las chicas?

_____

4. ¿Qué es posible hacer en la Pequeña Habana de Miami?

_____

5. ¿Qué es posible hacer en El Mercado de San Antonio?

_____

Conexión personal

What activities are most popular among students in your city or town? Fill in the name of your city in the center circle and write what activities students like to do in the outer circles.

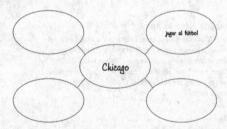

jugar al fútbol

Chicago

¿Comprendiste?
Comprehension questions check your understanding and provide the opportunity to practice new vocabulary words.

Conexión personal
These short writing activities will help you connect the information and events in the selections with your own life and interests.

Literatura adicional

Notes in the margins make literature from the Spanish-speaking world accessible and help you read works by famous authors such as Pablo Neruda.

Reading Strategy
This feature provides reading tips and strategies that help you effectively approach the material.

What You Need to Know
This section provides a key to help you unlock the selection so that you can understand and enjoy it.

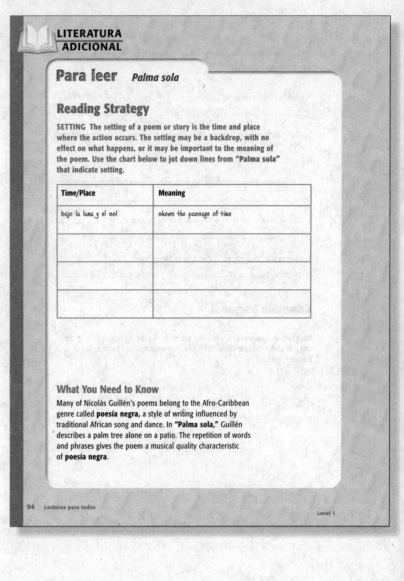

LITERATURA ADICIONAL

Para leer *Palma sola*

Reading Strategy

SETTING The setting of a poem or story is the time and place where the action occurs. The setting may be a backdrop, with no effect on what happens, or it may be important to the meaning of the poem. Use the chart below to jot down lines from "Palma sola" that indicate setting.

Time/Place	Meaning
bajo la luna y el sol	shows the passage of time

What You Need to Know

Many of Nicolás Guillén's poems belong to the Afro-Caribbean genre called **poesía negra,** a style of writing influenced by traditional African song and dance. In **"Palma sola,"** Guillén describes a palm tree alone on a patio. The repetition of words and phrases gives the poem a musical quality characteristic of **poesía negra.**

94   Lecturas para todos

Level 1

READING TIP Read the poem aloud. Let punctuation show you where to stop or pause. How many sentences are there in the poem? A capital letter begins each one. Write your answer on the line below.

APUNTES

MÁRCALO ➤ ANÁLISIS
Remember that **personification** is the attribution of human characteristics to an object, animal, or idea. Pablo Neruda uses personification to give life to foods. Find and circle examples of personification in the poem. Which foods are personified? Write your answer on the lines below.

CHALLENGE Why would the street be filled with tomatoes? **(Draw Conclusions)**

Sobre el autor

Pablo Neruda nació en Parral, Chile. Su verdadero nombre era Ricardo Neftalí Reyes. Estudió pedagogía en francés en la Universidad de Chile. Allí conoció a Albertina Azócar. A ella le dedica los primeros poemas de *Veinte poemas de amor y una canción desesperada* (1924). Para Neruda, todo puede ser poesía. En sus famosas *Odas elementales* escribió versos para el tomate, el átomo, un reloj, la pobreza y la soledad. Pablo Neruda fue diplomático en varios países de Europa y en México. En 1971 obtuvo el Premio Nobel de Literatura.

~~~~~~~~~~

Oda al tomate

La calle
se **llenó** de tomates,
mediodía,
verano,
5 la luz
se parte[1]
en dos
mitades
de tomate,
10 corre
por las calles
el jugo.

[1] is split

PALABRAS CLAVE
llenar   *to fill*   la mitad   *half*

Sobre el autor
Each literary selection begins with a short author biography that provides cultural context.

Reading Tips
Useful, specific reading tips appear at points where language is difficult.

MÁRCALO ➤ Análisis
This feature encourages you to focus on one aspect of literary analysis as you read.

Challenge
These activities help keep you challenged, even after you have grasped the basic concepts of

Academic and Informational Reading

This section helps you read informational material and prepare for other classes and standardized tests.

Varied Types of Readings

The wide variety of academic and informational selections helps you access different types of readings and develop specific techniques for those reading types.

Academic and Informational Reading

In this section you'll find strategies to help you read all kinds of informational materials. The examples here range from magazines you read for fun to textbooks to bus schedules. Applying these simple and effective techniques will help you be a successful reader of the many texts you encounter every day.

Skill Development

These activities offer graphic organizers, Mark It Up features, and other reading support to help you comprehend and think critically about the selection.

Test Preparation for All Learners

Lecturas para todos offers models, strategies, and practice to help you prepare for standardized tests.

Test Preparation Strategies

- Successful test taking
- Reading test model and practice—long selections
- Reading test model and practice—short selections
- Functional reading test model and practice
- Revising-and-editing test model and practice
- Writing test model and practice
- Scoring rubrics

APUNTES

READING STRATEGIES FOR ASSESSMENT

Find the main idea and supporting details. Circle the main idea of this article. Then underline the details that support the main idea.

Use context clues. To discover what a "pack animal" is, study the words and phrases around it. Which phrase helps define it?

Notice important details. Underline the details that explain why alpaca wool is so desirable.

Reading Test Model
SHORT SELECTIONS

DIRECTIONS "Warmth from the Andes" is a short informative article. The strategies you have just learned can also help you with this shorter selection. As you read the selection, respond to the notes in the side column.

When you've finished reading, answer the multiple-choice questions. Use the side-column notes to help you understand what each question is asking and why each answer is correct.

Warmth from the Andes

Southeastern Peru and Western Bolivia make up a geographic region called the *Altiplano*, or High Plateau. This largely desolate mountainous area is home to one of the most economically important animals in South America—the alpaca.

The alpaca is related to the camel and looks somewhat like another well-known South American grazing animal, the llama. Alpacas live at elevations as high as 16,000 feet. At such altitudes, oxygen is scarce. Alpacas are able to survive because their blood contains an unusually high number of red blood corpuscles, the cells that carry oxygen throughout the body.

For several thousand years, the Native Americans of the region have raised alpacas both as pack animals for transporting goods and for their most important resource—wool. Alpaca wool ranges in color from black to tan to white. It is lightweight yet strong and resists moisture. Also, it is exceptionally warm. Alpaca wool is much finer than the

Level 1

Revising-and-Editing Test Model

DIRECTIONS Read the following paragraph carefully. Then answer the multiple-choice questions that follow. After answering the questions, read the material in the side columns to check your answer strategies.

¹Madrid, the capital of Spain. ²It is home to one of that nations cultural treasures—the Prado museum. ³The building was constructed in the late eighteenth century as a museum of natural science. ⁴Then they decided to change it to an art museum in 1819 and it has more than 9,000 works of art. ⁵The museum is located on a street called the Paseo del Prado. ⁶Their are many famous paintings they're, including works by El Greco, Velázquez, and Goya.

READING STRATEGIES FOR ASSESSMENT

Watch for common errors. Highlight or underline errors such as incorrect spelling or punctuation; fragments or run-on sentences; and missing or misplaced information.

ANSWER STRATEGIES

1. Which sentence in the paragraph is actually a fragment, an incomplete thought?

   A. sentence 5

   B. sentence 3

   C. sentence 1

   D. sentence 4

   > Incomplete sentences. A sentence is a group of words with a subject and a verb that expresses a complete thought. If either the subject or the verb is missing, the group of words is an incomplete sentence.

2. In sentence 2, which of the following is the correct possessive form of *nation*?

   A. nation's

   B. nations's

   C. nations'

   D. nations

   > Possessive nouns. In sentence 2, the word *nation* is singular. So, it takes the singular possessive form.

Writing Test Model

DIRECTIONS Many tests ask you to write an essay in response to a writing prompt. A writing prompt is a brief statement that describes a writing situation. Some writing prompts ask you to explain *what, why,* or *how.* Others ask you to convince someone of something.

As you analyze the following writing prompts, read and respond to the notes in the side columns. Then look at the response to each prompt. The notes in the side columns will help you understand why each response is considered strong.

Prompt A

Some child-rearing experts believe that young people should be kept busy after school and on the weekends with a variety of structured activities, such as music lessons, sports, dance classes, and so on. Others say that young people today have been "overscheduled" and need more time to themselves—to read, think about the future, and even just to daydream.

Think about your experiences and the way your non-school time is structured. Do you think lots of structure, more personal time, or a combination of the two is most beneficial to young people? Remember to provide solid reasons and examples for the position you take.

ANALYZING THE PROMPT

Identify the focus. What issue will you be writing about? Circle the focus of your essay in the first sentence of the prompt.

Understand what's expected of you. First, circle what the prompt asks you to do. Then identify your audience. What kinds of details will appeal to this audience?

Strong Response

Today was a typical day for my little brother Jeff. He got up at five o'clock to go to the local ice rink for hockey practice. Then he was off to school. At the end of the school day,

ANSWER STRATEGIES

Capture the reader's interest. The writer begins by describing a typical busy day in his younger brother's life.

Para leer   *¿Qué te gusta hacer?*

Reading Strategy

USE A JUDGMENT LINE On the line, list all the activities in the survey according to their popularity.

Least popular

Most popular

What You Need to Know

A dual-language school is a school where two languages are spoken. Classes in all subjects may be taught in either language. Students at the school featured in this survey speak Spanish and English. See whether their interests are similar to your own.

This is a survey about what students like to do in their free time. It was conducted among students at a dual-language school in Florida.

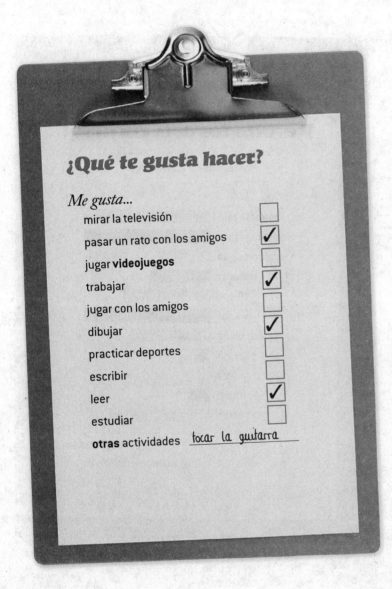

¿Qué te gusta hacer?

Me gusta...

mirar la televisión	☐
pasar un rato con los amigos	☑
jugar **videojuegos**	☐
trabajar	☑
jugar con los amigos	☐
dibujar	☑
practicar deportes	☐
escribir	☐
leer	☑
estudiar	☐
otras actividades	*tocar la guitarra*

READING TIP Many words in Spanish use accent marks to place stress on a particular syllable. Say some of the words with accent marks aloud, placing the stress on the accented syllable. This will help you get a feel for how the words sound, as well as how they look.

CHALLENGE Imagine you have received funds to create two new student clubs at the school featured in the survey. What types of clubs would you create and why? (Draw Conclusions)

_____

_____

_____

_____

_____

_____

_____

_____

_____

_____

_____

_____

_____

_____

_____

_____

_____

PALABRAS CLAVE
el videojuego *videogame*   **otro(a)** *other*

Look through the list of activities
and circle the ones that you
might do for a school assignment
or project. Underline the ones
you would do just for fun.

READER'S
SUCCESS
STRATEGY   Use the graph of
the survey results to help
you easily pick out which
activities were most popular
and which were least
popular.

A pensar...

What activities did all 25
students enjoy? Were there any
that no students checked off on
the survey? **(Explain)**

Resultados de la encuesta

25 estudiantes respondieron[1] a las 11
categorías o actividades.

Actividades

mirar la tele
pasar un rato
videojuegos
trabajar
jugar
dibujar
deportes
escribir
leer
estudiar
otras

5   10   15   20   25
Número de estudiantes

―――――
[1] replied

PALABRAS CLAVE
el resultado   *result*   **la categoría**   *category*
la encuesta   *survey*

Vocabulario de la lectura

Palabras clave

la categoría *category*

la encuesta *survey*

otro(a) *other*

el resultado *result*

el videojuego *videogame*

A. Complete each sentence with the correct form of a **Palabra clave**.

1. ¿Te gusta más jugar con los amigos o jugar _____?

2. La _____ tiene *(has)* información sobre *(about)* las actividades de los estudiantes.

3. A los estudiantes les gusta mirar la televisión, pasar un rato con

los amigos y hacer _____ actividades.

4. Según *(According to)* los _____ de la encuesta, a todos los estudiantes les gusta dibujar.

5. En la encuesta «¿Qué te gusta hacer?», «leer» es una _____.

B. Circle the word that is most different from the other words in each category.

1. las encuestas, la televisión, los videojuegos

2. los videojuegos, los números, los resultados

3. dibujar, leer, otras

4. las encuestas, la guitarra, las categorías

5. los estudiantes, los resultados, los amigos

¿Comprendiste?

1. How many students took the survey?

_____

2. What are the three most popular activities?

_____

3. What are the three least popular activities?

_____

4. How many students enjoyed "other" activities?

_____

5. Would you get the same results if you used the survey with your classmates? Give specific reasons why or why not.

_____

_____

_____

Conexión personal

Using the survey on the previous page, interview five classmates about their favorite activities. Then make a list of the five most popular activities and how many students like each one. Are your survey results similar to or different from the ones in the reading?

Actividades	Número de estudiantes

Para leer   *Saludos desde San Antonio y Miami*

Reading Strategy

MAKE A COMPARISON CHART Use the chart to compare San Antonio and Miami.

	San Antonio	Miami
Sitios de interés		
Actividades		
Comida		

What You Need to Know

When you think of Spanish-speaking people or cultures, you may imagine Spain or Mexico. However, did you know that Spanish is the second most widely spoken language in the United States? You don't have to travel far to find elements of Spanish-speaking culture or to hear people conversing in Spanish. In the following reading, you will learn about two U.S. cities where you would likely meet many Spanish speakers.

READING TIP As you learn Spanish, you will be able to recognize many Spanish words that look and sound like English words. These words are called cognates. Make a list of all of the cognates you can find in the reading and what they mean in English.

_____

_____

_____

_____

_____

READER'S SUCCESS STRATEGY As you read, compare the descriptions of each city with the photos you see. What elements of each city's description are pictured?

_____

_____

_____

_____

_____

_____

Saludos desde San Antonio y Miami

En San Antonio, Texas, **hay** parques de diversiones, museos y están el Paseo del Río y el Álamo. Después de las clases, a los chicos y a las chicas les gusta pasar un rato con
5 los amigos en El Mercado, donde es posible escuchar música de los mariachis y comer **comida** típica mexicana.

El Álamo en San Antonio, Texas

PALABRAS CLAVE
hay _there is, there are_   **la comida** _food_

Andar en patineta en Miami, Florida

MÁRCALO ⟩ **GRAMÁTICA**

You can recognize verbs in Spanish because they end **-ar**, **-er**, or **-ir**. These verbs are in the infinitive form. They are the equivalent of "to do…" in English. For example, **comer** means "to eat." In the boxed text, underline all the verbs in the infinitive.

A pensar…

How are the two cities described in the article similar to or different from the area where you live? **(Compare and Contrast)**

_____

_____

_____

_____

_____

_____

_____

CHALLENGE Do you think it would be more interesting to visit San Antonio or to visit Miami? Make a list of the features that you find most attractive in the city of your choice. **(Evaluate)**

_____

_____

_____

_____

_____

_____

_____

5

En Miami, Florida, si hace buen tiempo, a los chicos y a las chicas les gusta andar en
10 patineta o montar en bicicleta. Después de las clases, a muchos chicos les gusta pasear con los amigos por la **Calle** Ocho, en la Pequeña Habana de Miami. ¡Es una pequeña Cuba en la Florida! Allí es posible comer sándwiches
15 cubanos y beber jugo de mango.

PALABRAS CLAVE
la calle *street*

Vocabulario de la lectura

Palabras clave

el (la) amigo(a) *friend*

la calle *street*

la chica *girl*

el chico *boy*

la comida *food*

hay *there is, there are*

pequeño(a) *little*

A. Match each **Palabra clave** with the word or words to which it is most closely related.

_____ **1.** calle

_____ **2.** comida

_____ **3.** chicos

_____ **4.** amigos

_____ **5.** pequeño

a. personas jóvenes

b. no grande

c. sándwiches y pizza

d. pasear y montar en bicicleta

e. personas con quienes te gusta pasar un rato

B. Complete each sentence with the correct form of a **Palabra clave.**

1. A los chicos de San Antonio les gusta pasar un rato con

los _____.

2. En Texas _____ una fortaleza *(fortress)*: el Álamo.

3. Una actividad en Miami es pasear por la _____ Ocho.

4. A los _____ y a las _____ les gusta
montar en bicicleta.

5. Hay _____ en la Pequeña Habana: sándwiches cubanos.

¿Comprendiste?

1. ¿Qué hay en San Antonio?

_____

2. ¿Qué les gusta hacer después de las clases a los chicos y a las chicas de San Antonio?

_____

3. Si hace buen tiempo en Miami, ¿qué les gusta hacer a los chicos y a las chicas?

_____

4. ¿Qué es posible hacer en la Pequeña Habana de Miami?

_____

5. ¿Qué es posible hacer en El Mercado de San Antonio?

_____

Conexión personal

What activities are most popular among students in your city or town? Fill in the name of your city in the center circle and write what activities students like to do in the outer circles.

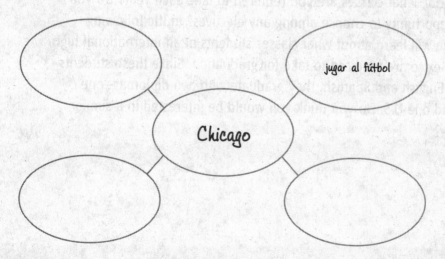

Para leer *Una escuela internacional en México*

Reading Strategy

USE WHAT YOU KNOW As you read the graduation requirements of Colegio Internacional, use what you know. Find words that sound and look somewhat similar to those in English—cognates like **ciencias** or **matemáticas**. Then use the context and what you already know to guess what **desarrollo humano** and **optativas** mean.

Cognates	Meanings

What You Need to Know

At your school, what classes are you required to take each year? Do you have the opportunity to choose among any electives? In the following reading, you will learn about what classes students at an international high school in Mexico are required to take for graduation. Since these students learn both English and Spanish, they graduate with two diplomas—one Mexican and one U.S. Do you think you would be interested in a similar opportunity?

Una escuela internacional en México

The following pages are from the student handbook for Colegio Internacional.

MANUAL DEL ESTUDIANTE

Estudiantes en el Colegio Internacional

«A mí me gusta mucho el **Colegio** Internacional. Las clases son muy buenas. Los maestros son trabajadores y muy inteligentes. Y los estudiantes son súper simpáticos. Siempre tenemos que trabajar mucho, pero... ¡¿dónde no?! Y también en la escuela hay muchas actividades después de las clases. ¡Es una escuela excelente!»

–Marta Ramos, estudiante

COLEGIO INTERNACIONAL
Colomos 2100 Colonia Providencia
Guadalajara, Jalisco 44640 México
http://www.asfg.mx

PALABRAS CLAVE
el colegio *high school*

READING TIP In informal Spanish, the word **súper** often precedes adjectives to add emphasis. For example, the handbook describes the students as **súper simpáticos** or *very nice*. The word *super* may sound a bit old-fashioned in English, but in Spanish it is commonly used among young people.

MÁRCALO **GRAMÁTICA**
Remember that all adjectives must agree with the noun they describe in both gender and number. In the boxed text, draw a line between each adjective you find and the noun it describes.

to quickly grasp what is
required to graduate from
the Colegio Internacional.
Identify the courses with the
greatest number of required
sections.

A pensar...

Do you think the course
requirements for this school
would leave students well
prepared to attend a university
in the U.S.? Why or why not?
(Make Judgments)

CHALLENGE Do you think you
would like to attend this school
if given the chance? Why or why
not? **(Evaluate, Connect)**

Requisitos para graduarse de bachillerato

A continuación[1], los **requisitos** para
graduarse con los dos **certificados:** el
certificado mexicano y el certificado
estadounidense.

Clase	Número de **unidades**
Inglés	4 unidades
Español	4 unidades
Matemáticas	4 unidades
Ciencias	4 unidades
Ciencias Sociales de México	1 unidad
Historia de México II	1 unidad
Geografía de México	1 unidad
Derecho[2]	1 unidad
Ciencias Sociales	3 unidades
Computación	0,5 unidades
Educación Física	0,5 unidades
Desarrollo Humano[3]	1 unidad
Optativas	2 unidades
Total	**27 unidades**

COLEGIO INTERNACIONAL

[1] **A...** Following are   [2] Law
[3] Human Development

PALABRAS CLAVE

el bachillerato   *high school*
  degree
el requisito   *requirement*
graduarse   *to graduate*

el certificado   *diploma*
la unidad   *credit*
la optativa   *elective*

Vocabulario de la lectura

Palabras clave

el bachillerato *high school degree*

el certificado *diploma*

el colegio *high school*

graduarse *to graduate*

el requisito *requirement*

la optativa *elective*

la unidad *credit*

A. Compare each pair of words below. If they mean the same thing, write **sí** in the blank; if they do not, write **no.**

1. la optativa; el requisito _____

2. el bachillerato; el certificado _____

3. la unidad; la optativa _____

4. terminar *(finish)* las clases; graduarse _____

5. el colegio; la escuela _____

B. Fill in each blank with the correct form of a **Palabra clave.**

En mi escuela, es posible _____ en tres años si *(if)* trabajas
(1)

mucho y estudias todos los días. Los _____ son estrictos: tienes
(2)

que tomar cuatro _____ de matemáticas, inglés, historia y
(3)

ciencias. Pero también hay _____: si eres artístico, hay clases de
(4)

arte y de música. Mi _____ es fantástico porque los profesores y
(5)

los estudiantes son muy inteligentes y estudiosos.

¿Comprendiste?

1. ¿Cuántas clases necesitas para los dos programas?

_____

2. ¿Cuántas unidades de matemáticas tienes que tomar?

_____

3. ¿Cuántas clases sobre *(about)* México hay en el programa?

_____

4. ¿Tienen que tomar clases de historia de Estados Unidos los estudiantes?

_____

5. ¿Cuántas unidades de optativas hay?

_____

Conexión personal

Use the Venn diagram to compare your classes with the classes that Colegio Internacional students take. In the left circle, list the classes that the students from the Colegio Internacional take that you do not. In the right circle, list the classes you take that are not offered at the Colegio Internacional. Write the classes you have in common in the center space, where the circles overlap.

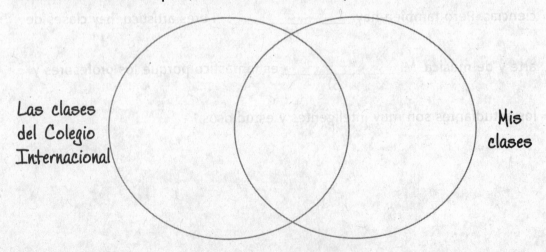

Las clases del Colegio Internacional

Mis clases

Para leer *Mi clase favorita*

Reading Strategy

USE THE TITLE The title *Mi clase favorita* helps you anticipate the contents of the reading. Write down the things that you would expect to find, then search for them.

Expected contents	Actual contents
El (La) maestro(a)...	
La clase...	

What You Need to Know

Think about your favorite class. Why do you like it? Is it because you earn good grades, because the material is especially interesting, or because you have a dynamic teacher? In the following compositions, you will read two students' descriptions of their favorite classes. As you will see, the students are from two different countries—Mexico and the Dominican Republic—and their favorite classes will help them prepare for rewarding and exciting careers in their own nations.

READING TIP You will notice that both students refer to their schools as **colegios**. While this word looks like the English word *college*, it actually means "high school." A Spanish word that looks like an English word but has a different meaning is called a false cognate.

▌▌▌MÁRCALO⟩ **GRAMÁTICA**
In this unit, you learned to conjugate regular **-ar** verbs in Spanish. In the boxed part of Tomás Gutiérrez Moreno's composition, circle the conjugated **-ar** verbs. Underline **-ar** verbs that are in the infinitive. *Hint: the infinitive of* **deseo** *is* **desear**.

READER'S SUCCESS STRATEGY Scan through the reading and use the following chart to help you identify some of the key details of each student's description.

Estudiante 1	Estudiante 2
Nombre	
País	
Clase(s) favorita(s)	
Profesión futura	

Mi clase favorita

Below are compositions by two finalists who entered the essay contest called "Mi clase favorita."

> Tomás Gutiérrez Moreno
> Colegio de la Providencia
> Guadalajara, México

> Mi nombre es Tomás Gutiérrez Moreno. Soy de Guadalajara, México. Estudio en el Colegio de la Providencia.
>
> La historia es muy interesante; es mi clase favorita. Me gusta mucho estudiar el **pasado** de México. Soy estudioso y siempre saco buenas notas en la clase.
>
> En la universidad deseo[1] estudiar historia. Deseo ser maestro y enseñar historia mexicana en Guadalajara.

[1] I wish to

Mural en la Biblioteca Central de la Universidad Nacional Autónoma de México en la Ciudad de México

PALABRAS CLAVE
el pasado *past, history*

María González
Colegio San Esteban
San Pedro de Macorís, República Dominicana

Me llamo María González. Soy de la República Dominicana. Estudio en el Colegio San Esteban.

Tengo dos clases favoritas: el inglés y el español. Deseo estudiar **idiomas** en Santo Domingo, la capital, y después, trabajar en mi país.

El **turismo** es muy **importante** para[2] la **economía** de la República Dominicana. Deseo trabajar en un hotel, en las famosas **playas** de Punta Cana o de Puerto Plata.

———
[2] for

Mural en la Universidad Nacional en Santo Domingo, República Dominicana

PALABRAS CLAVE

el idioma *language*
el turismo *tourism*
importante *important*

la economía *economy*
la playa *beach*

A pensar...

1. What plans and characteristics do Tomás and María have in common? **(Compare and Contrast)**

_____
_____
_____
_____
_____

2. What does María say is important for the economy of the Dominican Republic, and why do you think this is so? **(Clarify, Analyze)**

_____
_____
_____
_____

CHALLENGE Consider the career plans of Tomás and María. Which of their future professions would you most like to have? Give the reasons for your choice. **(Make Judgments)**

_____
_____
_____
_____
_____

Vocabulario de la lectura

Palabras clave

la economía *economy*
el idioma *language*
importante *important*
interesante *interesting*

el pasado *past, history*
la playa *beach*
el turismo *tourism*

A. Match each **Palabra clave** with the word or phrase to which it is most closely related.

_____ **1.** el pasado

_____ **2.** interesante

_____ **3.** el idioma

_____ **4.** el turismo

_____ **5.** la playa

a. visitar un país

b. la historia

c. no aburrido

d. el sol y el agua

e. el español y el inglés

B. Fill in the appropriate **Palabra clave** in each sentence. Then use the numbered letters to reveal the name of a tourist destination you might like to visit one day.

1. En la clase de historia nosotros estudiamos el __ __ __ __ __ __.

       1   9

2. El __ __ __ __ __ __ __ es muy importante en mi país; a muchas

    5 2 4
personas les gusta visitar las playas.

3. Si (*If*) te gusta sacar buenas notas, es __ __ __ __ __ __ __ __ __

                                              6   11   10
estudiar mucho.

4. A mis amigos y a mí nos gusta pasear en la __ __ __ __ __, cerca del

                                             7 8
agua.

5. El presidente habla de los problemas que tiene
la __ __ __ __ __ __ __ __ del país.

 3

__ __ __ __ __ __ __ __ __ __ __
1 2 3 4 5 6   7 8 9 10 11

¿Comprendiste?

1. ¿Dónde estudia Tomás?

_____

2. ¿Cómo es Tomás?

_____

3. ¿De dónde es María?

_____

4. ¿Qué le gusta estudiar más a María?

_____

5. ¿Dónde desea trabajar María? ¿Qué desea ser Tomás?

_____

Conexión personal

Use the compositions as a model to write your own essay about your favorite class. Include where you are from, where you study, what kind of student you are, what your favorite class is, and what you want your profession to be **(Deseo ser…)**. You may need to use a dictionary or ask your teacher how to say the name of your desired profession in Spanish.

Para leer *¡A comprar y a comer!*

Reading Strategy

DON'T TRANSLATE; USE PICTURES! Sketch and label pictures of the foods and beverages on the shopping list. Below each picture, write the brand or type of item you can buy at Supermercados La Famosa.

café	huevos	leche condensada	jugo de china
_____	_____	_____	_____
pan	yogur	jugo de piña	jamón de sándwich
_____	_____	_____	_____
queso de sándwich	uvas	manzanas	jamón ovalado
_____	_____	_____	_____

What You Need to Know

Next time you're in a grocery store, check out where items in the produce section came from. Most likely, you will find that several types of fruit have been imported from Central or South America. What else might the people in these regions eat? Though it may surprise you, if you went to the supermarket in a Latin American country, you would likely see many of the same items and brand names that you see at your local store.

¡A comprar y a comer! 🎧

The following is a supermarket circular from Supermercados La Famosa and a shopping list.

READING TIP When looking at an advertisement in a different language, try to distinguish brand names from other words. Most brand names do not need to be translated, so you can concentrate on the other words in the reading. Usually, brand names are capitalized.

READER'S SUCCESS STRATEGY Compare the items on the grocery list to the items in the advertisement, checking off each item as you find it. Use the pictures to help you.

SUPERMERCADOS LA FAMOSA

TENEMOS BUENOS **PRECIOS** Y PRODUCTOS SUPERIORES

Hamburguesas El bohío, 1.5 lbs.
$1.29

$1.79
Queso americano de sándwich Vitarroz 12 oz.[1]

Jamón de sándwich Astor
$1.79/LB.[2]

Uvas de California
$1.59/LB.

Yogur de mango La Yogurt
.59¢

$1.29
Queso crema La Cremosa 8 oz.

Leche condensada La Fe 14 oz.
.99¢

[1] **onzas** = ounces   [2] **libra** = pound

PALABRAS CLAVE

el precio *price*   **el queso crema** *cream cheese*

Look over the grocery list and circle the items that are dairy products. Underline the products that are fruits or that contain fruit.

A pensar...

1. If you buy 1 pound of grapes and 2 pounds of apples at Supermercados La Famosa, on which fruits will you spend more money? **(Draw Conclusions)**

_____

_____

2. Do you think the items on the grocery list represent a balanced and healthy diet? Why or why not? **(State an Opinion)**

_____

_____

_____

_____

CHALLENGE If you were to prepare a breakfast or lunch for yourself and a friend using the items from the grocery list, what would you make? Be creative! **(Evaluate)**

_____

_____

_____

_____

_____

Huevos del país $1.19[3]

Jamón ovalado Hak 5 lbs. $9.99

Manzanas rojas .79¢/LB.

Jugo de china Valemil 64 oz. $2.69

Jugo de piña Tropical, de concentrado 12 oz. .99¢

Pan de sándwich Club 24 oz. $1.69

Café El Morro 16 oz. $3.49

Pan Criollo 1 lb. $1.29

Precios válidos el viernes, el sábado y el domingo.

[3] En Puerto Rico usan dólares estadounidenses

Lista de compras

café

huevos

leche condensada

jugo de china

pan

yogur

cereal

jamón de sándwich

queso de sándwich

uvas

manzanas

PALABRAS CLAVE

del país _local, domestic_
rojo(a) _red_
la china _orange_

la piña _pineapple_
el pan criollo _French-style bread_
válido(a) _good, valid_

Level 1

Vocabulario de la lectura

Palabras clave

la china *orange*

del país *local, domestic*

el pan criollo *French-style bread*

la piña *pineapple*

el precio *price*

el queso crema *cream cheese*

rojo(a) *red*

válido(a) *good, valid*

A. Complete each sentence with the correct form of a **Palabra clave.**

1. En Supermercados La Famosa venden manzanas _____.

2. Tengo ganas de comer un sándwich de jamón; necesito comprar

   jamón y _____.

3. Los huevos no son importados (*imported*); son _____.

4. Las _____ son nutritivas porque tienen mucha vitamina C.

5. Venden dos quesos: el queso de sándwich y el _____.

B. Look at each group of words and circle the word that is not related.

1. queso crema, jamón, leche

2. precio, cereal, pan criollo

3. válido, bueno, del país

4. naranja, piña, china

5. café, jugo de china, hamburguesa

¿Comprendiste?

1. ¿Qué hay en la lista que no está en la circular?

_____

2. ¿Qué venden los Supermercados La Famosa que no está en la lista?

_____

3. ¿Qué frutas hay en la lista?

_____

4. ¿Qué comidas en la lista son para el desayuno?

_____

5. ¿En qué país está el supermercado?

_____

Conexión personal

If you had $10 to spend at Supermercados La Famosa, what would you purchase? Make a list of what you would buy and the amount you would spend on each item. Make sure you don't spend more than you have!

Comidas y bebidas	Precios

Para leer   *La quinceañera*

Reading Strategy

COMPARE AND CONTRAST Use the Venn diagram to compare the **quinceañera** celebrations of Peru and Puerto Rico.

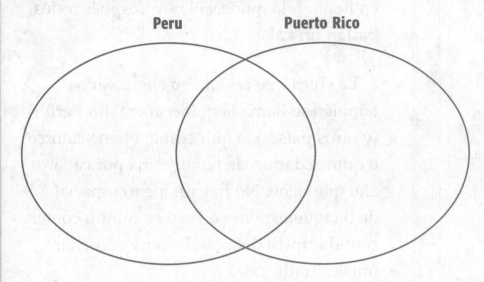

Peru   Puerto Rico

What You Need to Know

American students often eagerly anticipate their sixteenth birthdays, when in many states they can get their driver's license. In Latin America, many young women look forward to their fifteenth birthday with much more excitement, for it involves a **quinceañera** celebration. The **quinceañera** combines elements of a birthday party, a prom, and a wedding. The birthday girl usually wears a white dress, participates in a religious ceremony, and is honored with a party including traditional dances, gifts, and toasts. For many young women, the **quinceañera** is a much-anticipated event that represents a transition from childhood to adulthood.

MÁRCALO > GRAMÁTICA

You have learned to conjugate regular **-ar, -er,** and **-ir** verbs in Spanish, as well as some irregular verbs. Look though the boxed text and underline all the conjugated verb forms you can find.

READER'S SUCCESS STRATEGY Look at the following list of items and place a check mark next to the ones that are part of a typical **quinceañera.**

☐ 1. un banquete

☐ 2. deportes

☐ 3. damas de honor

☐ 4. una ceremonia religiosa

☐ 5. animales

☐ 6. música

☐ 7. un brindis

A pensar...

What elements of the **quinceañera** have you seen in celebrations you have attended in the United States? **(Connect)**

_____

_____

_____

_____

_____

_____

La quinceañera

La **fiesta** de quinceañera es muy popular en muchos países de Latinoamérica. Es similar al *Sweet Sixteen* de Estados Unidos. Muchas veces hay una ceremonia religiosa y una fiesta
5 con **banquete.** En la fiesta hacen un **brindis** en honor a la quinceañera y después todos **bailan** un vals[1].

La chica que celebra su cumpleaños también se llama la quinceañera. En Perú
10 (y otros países) la quinceañera tiene catorce o quince damas de honor[2]: una por cada[3] año que tiene. No hay un menú especial de banquete, pero en Perú es común comer comida **típica** del país, bailar y escuchar
15 música tradicional.

---

[1] waltz   [2] **damas...** maids of honor   [3] **por...** for each

Comidas tradicionales: lomo saltado, chupe, mondongo y guiso

PALABRAS CLAVE
la fiesta *party*
el banquete *banquet*
el brindis *toast*

bailar *to dance*
típico(a) *typical, traditional*

Una quinceañera en Puerto Rico con familia y amigos

A pensar...

What are some of the unique characteristics of a **quinceañero** in Puerto Rico? **(Summarize)**

_____

_____

_____

_____

En Puerto Rico, la celebración se llama el quinceañero. Muchas veces las chicas tienen la **gran** fiesta en su cumpleaños número dieciséis (por influencia del *Sweet Sixteen*) y no en el
20 cumpleaños de los quince años.

En el banquete de una quinceañera de Puerto Rico es normal comer comida típica del país, como arroz con pollo[4]. Todos bailan y escuchan música del Caribe: salsa,
25 merengue, reggaetón y el hip-hop cubano.

---
[4] **arroz...** chicken and rice dish

CHALLENGE How do you think the **quinceañera** feels on the day of her celebration? Use the word web below to list as many emotions as you can. **(Visualize, Infer)**

La quinceañera: emociones

PALABRAS CLAVE
gran *large, great*

Vocabulario de la lectura

Palabras clave

bailar   *to dance*

el banquete   *banquet*

el brindis   *toast*

el cumpleaños   *birthday*

la fiesta   *party*

gran   *large, great*

típico(a)   *typical, traditional*

A. Complete the crossword puzzle using **Palabras clave.**

Horizontal

1. una fiesta con mucha comida rica

3. una celebración con amigos o familia en una ocasión especial

Vertical

1. Necesitas música para...

2. tradicional

4. el aniversario del nacimiento de una persona

B. Fill in each blank with the correct form of a **Palabra clave.**

El sábado es la _____ de quinceañera de mi hermana.
                    (1)

Hay una ceremonia religiosa, y después vamos a la fiesta. Antes de comer,

hay un _____ a la salud *(health)* de mi hermana. Luego hay un
         (2)

banquete con comida _____ de Perú. Después de comer, todos
                      (3)

nosotros _____ con música tradicional. Mi hermana está muy
          (4)

contenta porque la quinceañera es un _____ día para ella.
                                       (5)

¿Comprendiste?

1. ¿Qué fiesta en Estados Unidos es similar a la fiesta de quinceañera?

_____

2. ¿Cuántas damas de honor tiene una quinceañera en Perú?

_____

3. ¿Cuándo tienen la fiesta las chicas de Puerto Rico?

_____

4. ¿Qué comen las personas en un banquete de quinceañera en Perú?

_____

5. ¿Qué tipo de música bailan las personas en un quinceañero en Puerto Rico?

_____

Conexión personal

Think about a special celebration in your future—it might be a birthday party, graduation party **(graduación)**, wedding **(boda)**, etc. Fill out the chart below with the information about how you imagine the party.

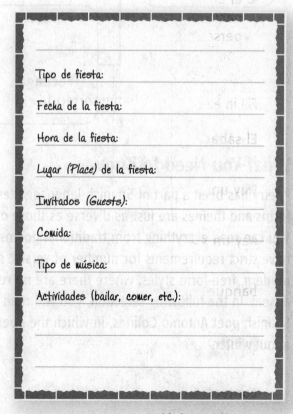

Tipo de fiesta:

Fecha de la fiesta:

Hora de la fiesta:

Lugar (Place) de la fiesta:

Invitados (Guests):

Comida:

Tipo de música:

Actividades (bailar, comer, etc.):

Para leer   *Las memorias del invierno*

Reading Strategy

FIND THE FEELINGS Find phrases that show the poet's feelings and write them in the chart. Write the feeling after each phrase.

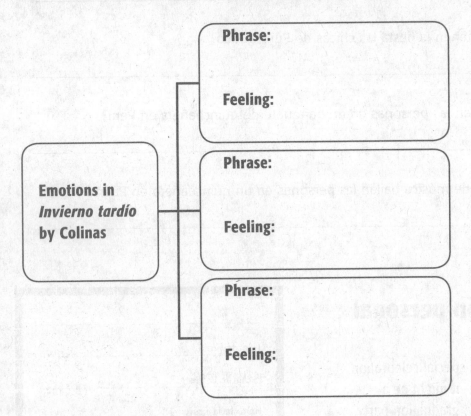

Emotions in
Invierno tardío
by Colinas

Phrase:

Feeling:

Phrase:

Feeling:

Phrase:

Feeling:

What You Need to Know

Poetry has been a part of Spanish-language literature for centuries, and its forms and themes are just as diverse as those of English-language literature. You can read everything from traditional poems, such as **sonetos,** which have strict requirements for number of verses, syllables, and rhyme, to modern, free-form styles, where there are no rules and rhyme is completely absent. In the following selection, you will read a poem by the modern Spanish poet Antonio Colinas, in which the poet reflects on his feelings about winter.

Las memorias del invierno

Antonio Colinas is a poet and novelist from León, in northern Spain. He published the following poem in 1988.

Antonio Colinas nació[1] en 1946 en La Bañeza, en la provincia de León, España. Escribe **poesía,** novelas, ensayos[2] y crítica. También estudia literatura italiana y la adapta al español. Su poesía ha ganado[3] muchos premios[4] en España, como el Premio Nacional de Literatura, en 1982. Ahora vive en Salamanca, España.

---

[1] was born   [2] essays
[3] **ha...** has won   [4] awards

PALABRAS CLAVE
la poesía *poetry*

MÁRCALO GRAMÁTICA
In this lesson, you learned to use direct object pronouns to avoid repetition. Circle the direct object pronoun in the boxed text, and write the word it replaces.

READING TIP Poets often use repetition to highlight the importance of a word or concept or give a sense of rhythm to their poetry. Look through the first stanza of the poem and see how many variations of the verb **nevar** you can find. As you read the poem, think about why the poet chooses to repeat this word.

READER'S SUCCESS STRATEGY Draw a sketch of the scene the poet describes. Include as many elements from the poem as you can. Be sure to include the poet himself.

1. To what does the poet compare his spirit? What do you think he means by these comparisons? **(Draw Conclusions)**

_____

_____

_____

_____

_____

2. In this poem, the poet creates a contrast between two seasons. What words or expressions are related to winter? What words or expressions are related to spring? **(Clarify)**

_____

_____

_____

_____

CHALLENGE If you had the opportunity to interview this poet and ask him three questions about himself or the poem, what would you ask? **(Question)**

_____

_____

_____

_____

_____

_____

Invierno tardío

No es increíble cuanto ven mis ojos[5]:

nieva sobre el almendro florido[6],

nieva sobre la **nieve**.

Este invierno mi **ánimo**

es como primavera temprana,

es como almendro florido

bajo la nieve.

Hay demasiado[7] frío

esta tarde en el mundo[8].

Pero **abro** la puerta a mi perro

y con él **entra** en **casa** calor,

entra la **humanidad.**

---

[5] **ven...** my eyes see   [6] **sobre...** on the flowery almond tree
[7] too much   [8] world

~56~

PALABRAS CLAVE

tardío(a) _late_	**entrar** _to enter_
la nieve _snow_	**la casa** _house_
el ánimo _spirit_	**la humanidad** _humanity_
abrir _to open_	

Vocabulario de la lectura

Palabras clave

abrir *to open*

el ánimo *spirit*

la casa *house*

entrar *to enter*

la humanidad *humanity*

el invierno *winter*

la nieve *snow*

la poesía *poetry*

la primavera *spring*

tardío(a) *late*

A. For each **Palabra clave** in the first column, find the phrase or definition in the second column that is closest in meaning. Write the corresponding letter in the blank.

_____ **1.** invierno

_____ **2.** nieve

_____ **3.** casa

_____ **4.** poesía

_____ **5.** primavera

a. un tipo de literatura

b. estación antes del verano

c. lugar (*place*) para vivir

d. estación en que hace frío

e. Es blanca y muy fría.

B. On the line next to each word pair, write whether the words are synonyms or antonyms. Synonyms are words with the same or similar meaning. Antonyms are words with opposite meanings.

1. humanidad – personas _____

2. abrir – cerrar _____

3. entrar – llegar _____

4. ánimo – espíritu _____

5. tardío – temprano _____

¿Comprendiste?

1. ¿De dónde es Antonio Colinas? ¿Qué escribe? ¿Dónde vive ahora?

_____

_____

2. ¿Dónde está la persona en el poema? ¿Qué mira?

_____

3. En tu opinión, ¿está triste o contenta la persona?

_____

4. ¿Piensas que el perro es un buen amigo? ¿Por qué?

_____

_____

Conexión personal

Use this word web to describe your favorite season. In the center circle, write the name of the season. In the surrounding circles, write the emotions, colors, weather, and activities you associate with that season.

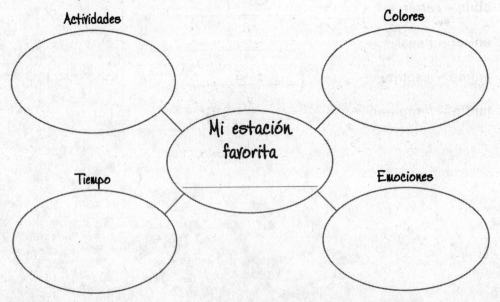

Actividades

Colores

Mi estación favorita
_____

Tiempo

Emociones

Para leer   *El fin de semana en España y Chile*

Reading Strategy

LIST ATTRACTIONS AND PLACES Use the table below to list attractions and the places where they can be found. Add two attractions to the table.

	conciertos	zoológico	botes		
Madrid					
Santiago de Chile					

What You Need to Know

What are your favorite weekend activities? You may enjoy spending time with friends, playing sports, going to concerts, or visiting local attractions. If so, you would likely have a great time visiting Madrid, Spain, or Santiago, Chile. Although they are thousands of miles apart, these two cities offer many similar attractions for both locals and tourists. In the following reading, you will learn more about some of the most popular places to find entertainment in each of these locations.

READING TIP In this reading, you will see two nouns that indicate city of origin: **madrileños** and **santiaguinos,** which refer to people from Madrid and Santiago, respectively. When you first encounter words like these, you can often figure out their meaning by their similarity to a place name. To whom might the nouns **argentinos** and **puertorriqueños** refer?

▌▌▌ MÁRCALO ◇ VOCABULARIO
Look through the boxed text and underline the vocabulary words for places around town.

READER'S SUCCESS STRATEGY Use the table below to list activities that people can do in each of the following popular sites in Madrid and Santiago.

Lugares	Actividades
Parque del Buen Retiro	
El Corte Inglés	
Cerro Santa Lucía	
Mercado Central	

El fin de semana en España y Chile

Los habitantes de Madrid, España, y Santiago de Chile hacen muchas actividades en el **fin de semana.** Van a parques, restaurantes, teatros, cines y otros lugares divertidos. También van de compras.

En Madrid hay muchos lugares interesantes para pasar los fines de semana. La Plaza Mayor tiene muchos cafés y restaurantes.

Hay un **mercado** de sellos[1] los domingos. El Parque del Buen Retiro es un lugar perfecto para descansar y pasear. En este parque hay **jardines,** cafés y un **lago** donde las personas pueden alquilar botes. Hay conciertos allí en el verano. Otro parque popular es la Casa de Campo. Hay un **zoológico,** una **piscina,** un parque de diversiones[2] y un lago para botes.

---

[1] stamps   [2] parque... amusement park

El Parque del Buen Retiro en Madrid

PALABRAS CLAVE
el fin de semana *weekend*
el mercado *market*
el jardín *garden*
el lago *lake*
el zoológico *zoo*
la piscina *pool*

La Plaza de Armas

Hay muchas tiendas en el centro. El **almacén** más grande es El Corte Inglés: allí los madrileños[3] pueden comprar ropa, comida y mucho más.

20

25

En Santiago de Chile, las personas pasan los fines de semana en muchos lugares. Siempre hay mucha actividad en la Plaza de Armas, la parte histórica de Santiago. Hay conciertos allí los domingos.

30

El parque del Cerro Santa Lucía es perfecto para pasear. Los santiaguinos[4] pueden ver jardines y el panorama de Santiago. El Cerro San Cristóbal en el Parque Metropolitano es un lugar favorito para comer, correr y montar en bicicleta. Hay jardines, piscinas, un zoológico, cafés y restaurantes en el parque.

35

Los santiaguinos van a tiendas en el centro y a centros comerciales como Alto Las Condes. En el Mercado Central pueden comprar pescado y frutas y comer en restaurantes con precios baratos[5].

40

45

Cerro San Cristóbal

[3] people of Madrid
[4] people of Santiago, Chile
[5] inexpensive

PALABRAS CLAVE
el almacén *department store*

A pensar...

If you were a travel agent, where would you recommend that each of the following people visit?
(Make Judgments)

a. Someone who loves nature

_____

_____

b. Someone who loves to shop for clothes

_____

_____

c. Someone who loves to try new foods but is on a tight budget

CHALLENGE Your Spanish class has received funds for a class trip to either Madrid or Santiago de Chile. You must choose which place you would rather visit and try to convince your classmates to agree with you. Give three reasons. **(Persuade)**

Vocabulario de la lectura

Palabras clave

el almacén   *department store*

el concierto   *concert*

el fin de semana   *weekend*

el jardín   *garden*   •

el lago   *lake*

el mercado   *market*

el parque   *park*

la piscina   *pool*

el restaurante   *restaurant*

el zoológico   *zoo*

A. Fill in each set of blanks with the correct form of a **Palabra clave.** Then unscramble the boxed letters to complete the sentence below the puzzle.

1. Tiene agua pero no es un lago, y no puedes usar un

   bote. __ ☐ __ ☐ __ __ __

2. Es una tienda muy grande con muchos departamentos

   diferentes. __ __ __ __ ☐ __ __

3. Es un lugar donde sirven platos principales y

   postres. __ __ __ ☐ __ __ __ __ __ __ ☐

4. Es un lugar donde puedes ver animales exóticos, como gorilas y

   elefantes. __ ☐☐ __ __ __ __ __ __ __

5. Aquí encontramos verduras como tomates y patatas, y otras

   plantas. __ __ ☐ __ __ ☐

   Para escuchar buena música, vamos al __ __ __ __ __ __ __ __ __ __ .

B. Write two sentences about weekend activities in Madrid and Santiago using two or more of the **Palabras clave.**

_____

_____

_____

_____

¿Comprendiste?

1. ¿Qué hay en la Plaza Mayor y la Plaza de Armas los domingos?

_____

2. ¿A qué parques van los madrileños y los santiaguinos?

_____

_____

3. ¿Dónde pueden ir de compras los habitantes de Santiago?

_____

_____

4. ¿Cómo se llama el almacén más grande en el centro de Madrid? ¿Qué venden allí?

_____

5. ¿Dónde pueden comer los habitantes de Santiago de Chile?

_____

_____

Conexión personal

Draw a simple map of your neighborhood or local area. Use symbols to identify interesting places to visit. Then write about activities people can do at each one.

Actividades
_____
_____
_____
_____
_____
_____
_____

Para leer   *Vivir en Ecuador*

Reading Strategy

USE A CHECKLIST AND EXPLAIN Use the checklist to show which place—apartment or house—is more useful for a single person, a small family, and a large family.

	el apartamento	la casa	¿Por qué?
Una persona			
Una familia pequeña			
Una familia grande			

What You Need to Know

Would you rather live in a house or in an apartment? In Spanish-speaking countries, just as in the U.S., many people choose to live in city apartments to have easy access to work and entertainment opportunities downtown, to take advantage of apartment facilities such as gyms or pools, or to be able to easily meet and get together with a variety of neighbors. Other people prefer the relative privacy and greater size of a house. On the following pages, you will see two real estate ads: one for an apartment in Quito, the capital city of Ecuador, and one for a house just outside Guayaquil, Ecuador's largest city. As you read, think about which dwelling you find more appealing and why.

Vivir en Ecuador

The following are an apartment brochure from Quito and a real-estate ad from Guayaquil.

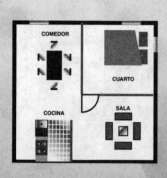

LAS CAMELIAS

COMUNIDAD RESIDENCIAL

EL QUITEÑO MODERNO

- Construcción antisísmica[1]
- Jardines comunales
- Sauna
- Gimnasio
- **Portero** de 24 horas
- Áreas verdes y recreativas
- Cerca de tiendas, supermercados y restaurantes

¿Quieres estar cerca de todo? El Quiteño Moderno está en un lugar muy conveniente.

Desde[2] el noveno piso puedes ver todo el centro.

Apartamento de 95 metros cuadrados[3] $65.000

RESIDENCIAS
PICHINCHA
AV. EL INCA, 32
TELÉFONO 244–5502

---

[1] earthquake-proof   [2] From   [3] square

READING TIP In Spanish, the use of commas and periods in numbers is the reverse of the English system. For example, English speakers write the numeral for one thousand, two hundred with a comma, (1,200). In contrast, Spanish speakers write 1.200. English speakers write one dollar and fifty cents as $1.50, whereas Spanish speakers write $1,50.

READER'S SUCCESS STRATEGY Use the following table to help you categorize some of the features of each dwelling. Put an "X" in the box if the dwelling has the feature.

El Quiteño Moderno	Cerro Santa Ana
gimnasio	
garaje	
cocina	
muchos cuartos	
portero	
lugar conveniente	

PALABRAS CLAVE
la comunidad *community*   **el (la) portero(a)** *door attendant*

A pensar...

Which residence do you think is a better value, and why? **(Evaluate)**

CHALLENGE In which residence would you rather live? Identify at least three specific reasons for your choice. **(Make Judgments)**

[||||| MÁRCALO > GRAMÁTICA
In this chapter, you learned about some of the different uses of the verbs **ser** and **estar**. Circle the form of **estar** in the boxed text and identify the reason **estar** is used.

Cerro Santa Ana
Comunidad **privada** de 18 residencias

Aquí puedes ir de compras o al cine y en unos minutos volver a tu casa cerca del **río** Guayas. Cerro Santa Ana es para las personas a quienes les gusta el aire puro tanto como un lugar urbano.

$130.000

Casa ultramoderna de dos pisos con acceso fácil a Guayaquil

- 4 cuartos
- 3 baños
- sala-comedor
- cocina
- oficina
- área de máquinas de lavar[4]
- 2 garajes

> La casa está en un lugar tranquilo pero no está muy lejos de Guayaquil. Puedes preparar la comida en el patio y hay **zonas** para practicar deportes.

Cerro Santa Ana | Escalón 68 | Teléfono 231–6687

---

[4] **maquinas...** washing machines

PALABRAS CLAVE
privado(a) *private*   **la zona** *area*
el río *river*

Vocabulario de la lectura

Palabras clave

el apartamento *apartment*

la casa *house*

la comunidad *community*

el cuarto *room; bedroom*

el jardín *garden*

el (la) portero(a) *door attendant*

privado(a) *private*

el río *river*

la zona *area*

A. Match each **Palabra clave** with the phrase to which it is most closely related. Write the corresponding letter in the blank.

_____ **1.** jardín

_____ **2.** cuarto

_____ **3.** zona

_____ **4.** portero

_____ **5.** comunidad

a. un lugar para dormir

b. lugar verde que tiene plantas

c. un área o una región

d. grupo de personas o casas

e. persona al lado de la puerta

B. Add the **Palabra clave** that is most closely related to each group.

1. no público, individual, _____

2. verde, plantas, _____

3. el agua, el lago, _____

4. más cuartos, más privada, _____

5. más pequeño, menos privado, _____

¿Comprendiste?

1. ¿Cómo es el apartamento y dónde está? ¿Y la casa?

_____

_____

_____

2. ¿Qué puedes hacer en los dos lugares?

_____

_____

_____

3. ¿Cuál es mejor para una familia, el apartamento o la casa? ¿Por qué?

_____

Conexión personal

Create an advertisement describing
your house or apartment building.
Draw a picture or floorplan in
the box. Then write five attractive
features of your home on the lines.

_____

_____

_____

_____

_____

_____

Para leer
Bailes folklóricos de Ecuador y Panamá

Reading Strategy

DRAW KEY ASPECTS Draw pictures of the sanjuanito and the tamborito. Label key aspects of your drawings. Then add more details by writing captions describing each dance.

Sanjuanito	Tamborito

_____   _____

_____   _____

What You Need to Know

In most Latin American countries, as in the United States, there is a great deal of ethnic diversity. The three main groups to which most Latin Americans can trace their ancestry are the indigenous peoples of the Americas, the Spanish, and the peoples of Africa. Over the years, these groups have mixed to create not only ethnic diversity, but a rich and exciting variety of cultural traditions, music, food, and dance. In the following reading, you will learn about some traditional dances in Ecuador and Panama.

Bailes folklóricos de Ecuador y Panamá

Los bailes folklóricos de Latinoamérica representan una combinación de culturas. Ayudan a formar una identidad nacional y continuar las tradiciones de las personas que
5 viven allí. A muchas personas de Ecuador y Panamá les gusta bailar cuando celebran fiestas.

Hay muchos **bailes** de **influencia indígena** en Ecuador. Uno de los bailes más populares se llama el sanjuanito. El sanjuanito tiene un
10 ritmo alegre[1] y es una buena representación de la fusión de culturas indígenas y españolas.

Para bailar, chicos y chicas forman un círculo y muchas veces bailan con **pañuelos** en las **manos**. Es posible ver el baile del
15 sanjuanito todo el año en celebraciones en casa, pero es más común durante el festival de San Juan en junio.

[1] **ritmo...** upbeat rhythm

Un baile tradicional en Mitad del Mundo, Ecuador

PALABRAS CLAVE
el baile dance
la influencia influence
indígena indigenous

el pañuelo scarf, handkerchief
la mano hand

Un baile folklórico, Ciudad de Panamá

En Panamá, es muy popular bailar salsa en fiestas o discotecas[2], pero el baile nacional
20 es el tamborito. El tamborito usa ritmos de influencia africana, pero también tiene orígenes indígenas y españoles.

Las personas bailan al sonido[3] de palmadas[4] y **tambores** africanos. El tamborito es popular
25 durante fiestas grandes y celebraciones regionales, como Carnaval. Para bailar en los festivales, las chicas llevan polleras (los vestidos tradicionales de Panamá) y los chicos llevan el dominguero (pantalones negros con
30 una camisa blanca).

---

[2] nightclubs [3] sound [4] handclaps

1. Have you ever seen a traditional cultural dance? If so, where and what was it like? If not, would you like to? **(Connect)**

_____

_____

_____

_____

2. Do you think the **sanjuanito** and **tamborito** will continue to be performed in the years to come? Why or why not? **(Predict)**

_____

_____

_____

_____

CHALLENGE Dance is one manner of preserving and passing on cultural traditions. What other art forms serve the same purpose? **(Connect, Activate Prior Knowledge)**

_____

_____

MÁRCALO VOCABULARIO
Look through the boxed text and circle the words that refer to clothing worn during the **tamborito.** Underline the words for instruments or sounds that are part of the dance.

PALABRAS CLAVE
el tambor *drum*

Vocabulario de la lectura

Palabras clave

bailar *to dance*

el baile *dance*

la fiesta *party*

indígena *indigenous*

la influencia *influence*

la mano *hand*

el pañuelo *scarf*

el tambor *drum*

A. Complete the crossword puzzle using **Palabras clave**.

Horizontal

2. Es una celebración.

4. La usas para escribir.

5. Es un artículo de ropa.

Vertical

1. El sanjuanito es un _____.

3. Un instrumento del tamborito es el _____.

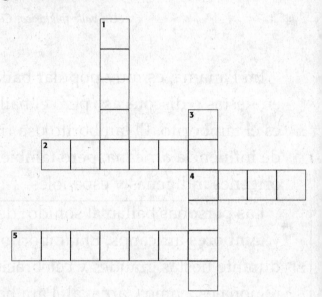

B. Choose three of the **Palabras clave** and write a sentence with each one.

_____

_____

_____

_____

¿Comprendiste?

1. ¿Por qué son importantes los bailes folklóricos de Latinoamérica?

_____

2. ¿Qué influencias culturales forman el baile del sanjuanito? ¿Y el tamborito?

_____

_____

3. ¿Qué artículos de ropa usan para bailar en Ecuador? ¿Y en Panamá?

_____

_____

4. ¿En qué tipo de fiestas bailan el sanjuanito y el tamborito?

_____

_____

5. ¿Cómo es el ritmo de los dos bailes?

_____

Conexión personal

Write an e-mail to a friend inviting him or her to a party with dancing at your house. Include what time your friend should come, what type of music and dancing there will be, and what else you and your friends will do at the party.

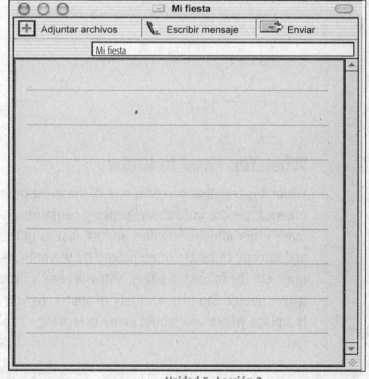

Para leer *Un club de deportes*

Reading Strategy

MAKE A MIND MAP Make a mind map of the sports club in Santo Domingo, showing everything the club offers. Add circles! Highlight the features you like most.

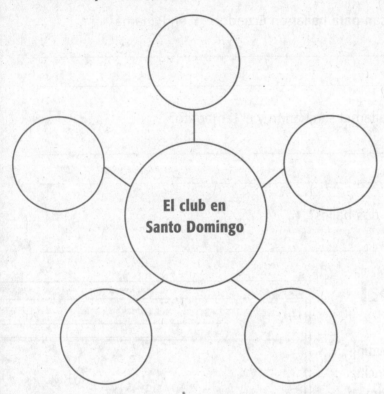

El club en
Santo Domingo

What You Need to Know

While it is true that soccer is one of the most popular sports in Latin America, people in Spanish-speaking countries also enjoy and participate in many other athletic activities. In fact, just as in the United States, local gyms and athletic clubs are often judged by the number of different activities they offer. On the following pages, you will read a brochure for an athletic club where people can play a variety of sports. As you read, try to decide if this is a place where you would enjoy exercising.

52   Lecturas para todos

Level 1

Un club de deportes

This is a brochure for a sports club in Santo Domingo.

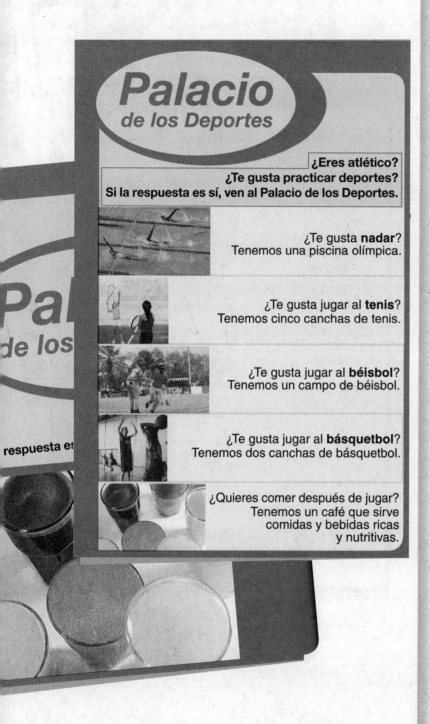

Palacio de los Deportes

¿Eres atlético?
¿Te gusta practicar deportes?
Si la respuesta es sí, ven al Palacio de los Deportes.

¿Te gusta **nadar**?
Tenemos una piscina olímpica.

¿Te gusta jugar al **tenis**?
Tenemos cinco canchas de tenis.

¿Te gusta jugar al **béisbol**?
Tenemos un campo de béisbol.

¿Te gusta jugar al **básquetbol**?
Tenemos dos canchas de básquetbol.

¿Quieres comer después de jugar?
Tenemos un café que sirve comidas y bebidas ricas y nutritivas.

PALABRAS CLAVE
nadar *to swim*
el tenis *tennis*
el béisbol *baseball*
el básquetbol *basketball*

A pensar...

1. Read the following statements about Palacio de los Deportes. If the statement is a fact, write an F in the blank. If it is an opinion, write O. **(Distinguish Fact from Opinion)**

_____ 1. El club tiene clases de tenis.

_____ 2. El club está en un lugar conveniente.

_____ 3. El equipo de voleibol es muy divertido.

_____ 4. Puedes ir al club los sábados.

CHALLENGE If offered a tour of the club, what questions would you ask the guide? Think of three questions. **(Question)**

_____

_____

_____

_____

_____

_____

_____

_____

_____

_____

_____

_____

Palacio de los Deportes

Para nuestros **socios...**

Si no sabes practicar los siguientes[1] deportes, tenemos clases de...

- **natación**
- tenis
- artes marciales
- **ejercicios** aeróbicos

Si quieres jugar con otras personas, hay equipos de...

- básquetbol
- béisbol
- **voleibol**

Horas

lunes a viernes	6:00 de la mañana a 9:00 de la noche
sábado	7:00 de la mañana a 6:00 de la tarde

Membresías
Hay membresías personales y familiares[2]. Puedes pedir la lista de los precios.

Dirección	**Teléfono**
Calle Mella, 100	(809) 583-1492
Santo Domingo	

---

[1] following   [2] family

PALABRAS CLAVE

el (la) socio(a)	*member*	**el voleibol**	*volleyball*
la natación	*swimming*	**la membresía**	*membership*
el ejercicio	*exercise*	**la dirección**	*address*

Vocabulario de la lectura

Palabras clave

el básquetbol *basketball*

el béisbol *baseball*

la dirección *address*

el ejercicio *exercise*

la membresía *membership*

nadar *to swim*

la natación *swimming*

el (la) socio(a) *member*

el tenis *tennis*

el voleibol *volleyball*

A. Complete each sentence with the correct form of a **Palabra clave.**

El Palacio de los Deportes está en Santo Domingo. Su _____ es

Calle Mella, 100. Si una persona quiere ser _____, tiene que

pagar una _____ personal o familiar. Para las personas a

quienes les gusta jugar con otras personas, hay equipos. También

pueden hacer _____ individuales, como la _____.

B. Fill in each set of blanks with the correct form of a **Palabra clave.** Then unscramble the boxed letters to complete the question below.

1. Si quieres tener una ☐ __ __ __ ☐☐ __ __ ☐ en el club de deportes, tienes que pagar.

2. En la piscina olímpica hay clases de __ ☐☐☐ __ __ __.

3. Una __ __ ☐☐ __ __ ☐ __ indica el lugar donde vive una persona.

4. Un ☐ __ ☐ __ __ tiene acceso a un club.

5. Para jugar al __ __ __ ☐ __ __ ☐, necesitas una pelota y un bate.

¿Quieres tomar clases de __ __ __ __ __ __ __ __ __ __ __ __ __ __ __?

¿Comprendiste?

1. ¿A qué puedes jugar en el Palacio de los Deportes?

_____

2. ¿Qué puedes hacer si no sabes nadar?

_____

3. Si queres jugar con un equipo, ¿a qué puedes jugar?

_____

4. ¿Puedes ir al club todos los días?

_____

5. ¿Qué tipo de membresías tiene el club?

_____

Conexión personal

What do you think an ideal sports club should offer? Think of classes, hours, memberships, etc. What would you name the ideal club? Write your ideas in the lines provided.

El club de deportes ideal tiene...

_____

_____

_____

_____

_____

_____

_____

_____

_____

_____

_____

Para leer *Dos atletas de alta velocidad*

Reading Strategy

CHART THE DATA In the chart below, record the following data for Félix and Daniela.

	País	Deporte	Medallas	Año(s) en que ganó
Félix				
Daniela				

What You Need to Know

Athletes from Spanish-speaking countries have competed in various Olympic sports since the beginning of the modern Olympic movement. In the 2000 and 2004 games, American athlete Félix Sánchez chose to represent the Dominican Republic, the country of his heritage. In the following reading, you will learn about Sánchez's quest for the gold, as well as the story of Daniela Larreal, a Venezuelan cyclist whose achievements have inspired many young athletes. As you will see, these two athletes were motivated not by fame and fortune, but by a desire to bring pride and recognition to their nations and cultures.

MÁRCALO **GRAMÁTICA**
In this lesson, you learned how to form the preterite of regular **-ar** verbs. Underline each preterite **-ar** verb you find in the boxed text.

READER'S SUCCESS STRATEGY Use a timeline like the one below to help you keep track of important events in the reading. Add four more events to the timeline.

2000 • 2000: Olympic games in Sydney. Sánchez comes in fourth

presente

Dos atletas de alta velocidad

Latinoamérica tiene una gran historia de deportes y de atletas ganadores. Algunos practican su deporte día y noche, en las calles y **pistas** que están muy lejos de los
5 aficionados y de las cámaras de televisión.

Félix Sánchez es uno de los atletas más dominantes en los 400 **metros** de **vallas**. Estadounidense de nacimiento, Sánchez decidió representar a la República
10 Dominicana, el país de sus padres, en competiciones internacionales. En los Juegos Olímpicos del 2000 en Sydney, Australia, Félix Sánchez llegó en cuarto lugar. Para tener motivación, Sánchez prometió[1] llevar el
15 **brazalete** que llevó en Sydney hasta[2] ganar una **medalla** de **oro**. Lo llevó por cuatro años. En los Juegos Olímpicos del 2004, ganó la

[1] promised [2] until

Félix Sánchez con la bandera dominicana

PALABRAS CLAVE
la pista   *track*
el metro   *meter*
la valla   *hurdle*

el brazalete   *bracelet*
la medalla   *medal*
el oro   *gold*

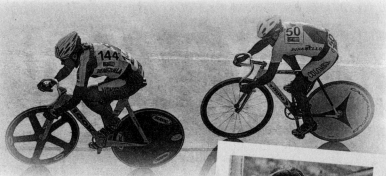

primera medalla de oro para la República Dominicana y se
20 hizo[3] héroe nacional. Después de ganar, el triunfante Sánchez caminó delante de
25 los aficionados con la bandera[4] dominicana en las manos.

Daniela Larreal y su medalla de oro

Muchas personas montan en bicicleta pero pocas van tan rápido como la ciclista venezolana Daniela Larreal. Ella ganó tres
30 medallas de oro en los Juegos Bolivarianos en el 2001. En el 2003, se hizo campeona de la Copa Mundial[5] de Ciclismo de Pista. En agosto del 2005, ella ganó otra medalla de oro en los Juegos Bolivarianos. Llegó
35 a los 500 metros con un tiempo de 35, 56 segundos. «Qué rico es **volver a** estar en unos Bolivarianos y ganar nuevamente otra medalla», comentó la campeona.

[3] became   [4] flag   [5] **Copa...** World Cup

PALABRAS CLAVE
volver + a + infinitive *to do (something) again*

A pensar...

What do you think of Félix Sánchez's decision to represent the Dominican Republic, even though he was born in the United States? **(Evaluate, State an Opinion)**

CHALLENGE You have the opportunity to interview Félix Sánchez or Daniela Larreal. Write the name of the person you will interview and list five questions you will ask in your interview. **(Question)**

Entrevista *(Interview)* con:

READING TIP The Juegos Bolivarianos are named for Simón Bolívar (1783–1830), a South American general who fought for South American independence from Spain. He is considered one of Latin America's greatest heroes.

Vocabulario de la lectura

Palabras clave

el brazalete *bracelet*

la medalla *medal*

el metro *meter*

el oro *gold*

la pista *track*

la valla *hurdle*

volver + a + infinitive *to do (something) again*

A. For each **Palabra clave** in the first column, find the phrase in the second column that best relates to it. Write the corresponding letter in the blank.

_____ **1.** el oro

a. una cosa que llevas en el brazo

_____ **2.** el brazalete

b. repetir, hacer otra vez

_____ **3.** la pista

c. objeto que le dan al ganador de una competición

_____ **4.** la medalla

d. un metal

_____ **5.** volver a hacer

e. un lugar para correr

B. Fill in each blank with the correct form of a **Palabra clave.**

1. Un _____ es una distancia corta.

2. Si una persona no corre en la calle, corre en una _____.

3. La campeona ganó una _____.

4. Félix Sánchez participa en competiciones de las _____.

5. La medalla de _____ es para la persona más rápida.

¿Comprendiste?

1. ¿Qué deporte practica Félix Sánchez? ¿Y Daniela Larreal?

_____

2. ¿Qué ganó Sánchez?

_____

3. ¿Qué ganó Larreal?

_____

_____

4. ¿Por qué representó Sánchez a la República Dominicana?

_____

5. Haz una comparación de los dos atletas. ¿Qué hacen? ¿De dónde son?

_____

_____

_____

Conexión personal

Write a short paragraph about your favorite sport to play or watch. Include information about why you like it and how often and with whom you play, practice, or watch it. Mention any medals or competitions you (or your favorite athlete in the sport) have won.

Mi deporte favorito

Para leer

Un cuestionario sobre las computadoras

Reading Strategy

USE A CAUSE-AND-EFFECT CHART Fill in the cause-and-effect chart for computer viruses.

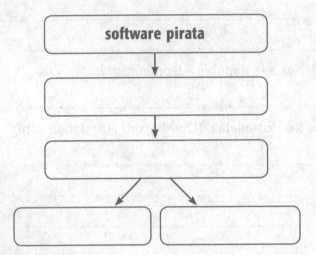

software pirata

What You Need to Know

Has your computer ever been the victim of a virus? If so, you are not alone. Since the first virus was created over 20 years ago, computer users all over the world have been tormented by these intruders. Spanish-language magazines and Web sites frequently deal with the topic of virus protection and prevention, in the hopes that users will educate themselves and avoid being a target. The following Web page uses a self-quiz to help readers assess their level of awareness. How much do you know about this important topic?

Un cuestionario sobre las computadoras

READING TIP This questionnaire contains many cognates and words that have been directly incorporated into Spanish from English. As you read, try not to worry about the words you don't know. Instead, focus on cognates, words borrowed from English, and words you do know to get a general idea of the information contained in the questionnaire.

Cuestionario: Protección para tu PC ✖

www.antivirus.ar

Cuestionario: Protección para tu PC

¿Qué pasa cuando un virus infecta tu computadora? El virus funciona como un borrador. Puede **destruir** tus **archivos.** Puede afectar tu acceso a Internet y el sistema del correo electrónico. Otras personas pueden ver tus datos personales. ¿Conoces las medidas[1] básicas que debes tomar como protección contra[2] los virus? Toma este cuestionario para saber.

1. **¿Cuál de los siguientes *no* es un método típico de propagación[3] de los virus?**

  A. programas que se **descargan** de Internet
  B. archivos adjuntos[4] a correos electrónicos
  C. la provisión de **datos** personales en un sitio Web no **seguro**
  D. software pirata

[1] measures   [2] against   [3] spreading   [4] attached

⫿⫿ MÁRCALO ⟩ VOCABULARIO
In this lesson, you learned many words related to technology and computer use. In the boxed text, circle the technology-related words.

READER'S SUCCESS STRATEGY Use a table like the one below to help you organize problems and solutions presented in this questionnaire. On the left, list problems caused by computer viruses. On the right, list protective measures people can take to avoid viruses.

Problemas de los virus	Protección contra los virus

PALABRAS CLAVE

destruir *to destroy*
el archivo *file*
descargar *to download*

los datos *information*
seguro(a) *safe, secure*

A pensar...

Why is the answer to question 2 "false"? **(Analyze)**

_____

_____

_____

_____

_____

_____

_____

CHALLENGE A friend of yours who is not very technologically savvy is planning to buy her first computer. She wants some advice on what to buy, what to do with the computer, and how to keep her computer safe from viruses. Give her three pieces of advice, using **tú** commands. **(Infer, Convince)**

_____

_____

_____

_____

_____

_____

_____

_____

_____

_____

Cuestionario: Protección para tu PC

 www.antivirus.ar

Cuestionario: Protección para tu PC

Centro de Protección

Introducción
Protege tu equipo
Recursos

2. Cierto o falso: Después de instalar software antivirus, la computadora está completamente **protegida**.
 A. cierto
 B. falso

3. ¿Qué es un firewall de Internet?
 A. una **contraseña** segura
 B. un artículo de asbesto que **protege** la computadora de las llamas[5]
 C. un candado[6] que puedes poner en la computadora para impedir acceso no autorizado
 D. software o hardware que ayuda a proteger la computadora contra **ataques** como los virus

---

HAZ CLIC

Respuestas correctas

1. C: la provisión de datos personales en un sitio Web no seguro
2. B: falso
3. D: software o hardware que ayuda a proteger la computadora contra ataques como los virus

---

[5] flames   [6] padlock

PALABRAS CLAVE
instalar _to install_   **proteger** _to protect_
protegido(a) _protected_   **el ataque** _attack_
la contraseña _password_

Level 1

Vocabulario de la lectura

Palabras clave

el archivo *file*

el ataque *attack*

la contraseña *password*

los datos *information*

descargar *to download*

destruir *to destroy*

instalar *to install*

proteger *to protect*

protegido(a) *protected*

seguro(a) *safe, secure*

A. Complete each analogy with one of the **Palabras clave.** In an analogy, the last two words must be related in the same way that the first two are related.

1. COMIDA : REFRIGERADORA : : la información : _____

2. MAESTRO : ENSEÑAR : : policía : _____

3. DISCO COMPACTO : QUEMAR : : programa : _____

4. GRANDE : PEQUEÑO : : peligroso : _____

5. SALIR : LLEGAR : : proteger : _____

B. Fill in each blank with the correct form of a **Palabra clave.**

Cuando usas la computadora, hay algunas reglas importantes. Si te conectas

a Internet, es importante _____ información o música de un sitio
                                    (1)
Web _____. Otras personas no deben tener acceso ni a tu correo
         (2)
electrónico ni a tus _____ personales. Entonces no debes
                              (3)
decirle a nadie tu _____ . Para proteger tu computadora contra
                          (4)
los _____ de los virus, debes instalar un software antivirus y
         (5)
usar un firewall.

¿Comprendiste?

1. ¿Por qué son peligrosos los virus?

_____

_____

2. ¿Cuáles son los métodos típicos de propagación de los virus?

_____

_____

3. ¿Cómo se llama el software o hardware que ayuda a proteger la computadora contra ataques como los virus?

_____

4. ¿Qué necesitas para tener acceso a algunos sitios Web?

_____

5. Si instalas un software antivirus, ¿pueden infectar tu computadora los virus?

_____

Conexión personal

Write your opinions about the advantages *(ventajas)* and problems of using a computer.

Ventajas	Problemas

Para leer *Museos excepcionales*

Reading Strategy

COMPARE MUSEUMS Use the table to compare the two museums by name *(nombre)*, location *(ubicación)*, focus *(enfoque)*, and exhibits *(exhibiciones)*.

	Aire libre	Instrumentos musicales
Nombre		
Ubicación		
Enfoque		
Exhibiciones		

What You Need to Know

Have you ever visited a museum? Even if you haven't visited them personally, you have most likely heard of famous U.S. museums such as the Metropolitan in New York City and the Smithsonian in Washington, D.C. Likewise, you may have heard of famous museums in Spanish-speaking countries, such as the Prado in Madrid, Spain. You may not know there are many smaller museums that provide an unusual and especially memorable experience for their visitors. The following reading discusses two of these exceptional museums. As you read, think about whether you would like to visit these places.

_____

_____

_____

_____

_____

_____

CHALLENGE You have received funds to open a special-interest museum related to a theme, activity, or event that is important to you. Describe what kind of museum you will establish and what it will contain. **(Extend)**

_____

_____

_____

_____

_____

_____

_____

_____

Museos excepcionales

¿**Q**ué imaginas cuando piensas en un museo? Muchas personas imaginan cuartos formales con **obras** de arte. Hay museos en Latinoamérica que celebran su cultura
5 y también dan una experiencia diferente, sin[1] tantas restricciones como un museo tradicional.

El Museo **al Aire Libre** no tiene ni puertas ni **paredes**, pero es uno de los museos más
10 populares de Buenos Aires. Está en el corazón de La Boca, una sección de Buenos Aires cerca del mar, en una calle pequeña que se llama el Caminito. Allí viven muchos artistas argentinos en sus famosas casas multicolores.

[1] without

El Museo al Aire Libre en Buenos Aires, Argentina

PALABRAS CLAVE
la obra *work*   **la pared** *wall*
al aire libre *open-air, outdoor*

El Museo de Instrumentos Musicales en La Paz, Bolivia

15 El Caminito sirve como un **marco** natural para diversas obras de arte: **pinturas**, **esculturas** y murales. Es posible caminar por la calle, ver obras de arte, comer en cafés, escuchar música y mirar a personas que bailan el tango.

20 La cultura boliviana, especialmente la música, tiene dos orígenes: indígena[2] y español. En el centro de La Paz, Bolivia, la calle Jaén tiene varios museos de arte donde puedes ver obras indígenas. El Museo de Instrumentos

25 Musicales es un poco diferente de los otros. En este museo interactivo, ¡puedes tocar algunos de los instrumentos! Allí hay exhibiciones de instrumentos **precolombinos,** instrumentos de viento y **tambores**. Puedes tocar instrumentos

30 como el charango, una guitarra pequeña de influencia española.

[2] indigenous

PALABRAS CLAVE
el marco *frame*
la pintura *painting*
la escultura *sculpture*

precolombino(a) *pre-Columbian*
el tambor *drum*

READING TIP As you already know, the verb **tocar** means "to play (an instrument)." It can also mean "to touch." In the phrase puedes **tocar algunos de los instrumentos,** both meanings of the verb make sense. Given that the museum is "interactive," which do you think is the best translation of the phrase: "you can play some of the instruments" or "you can touch some of the instruments"?

|||**MÁRCALO**⟩ **GRAMÁTICA**
You have already learned about the use of the personal **a**. Circle the personal **a** in the boxed text and write a sentence below explaining why it is used.

_____

_____

_____

READER'S SUCCESS STRATEGY Scan through the reading and mark which of the two museums mentioned has each of the characteristics listed below. Write **MAL** next to characteristics of the Museo al Aire Libre and **MIM** next to characteristics of the Museo de Instrumentos Musicales.

1. _____ Está en Buenos Aires.
2. _____ Puedes tocar el charango.
3. _____ Hay exhibiciones de instrumentos precolombinos.
4. _____ No hay ni puertas ni paredes.
5. _____ Hay personas que bailan el tango.

Vocabulario de la lectura

Palabras clave

al aire libre   *open-air, outdoor*

la escultura   *sculpture*

el marco   *frame*

el museo   *museum*

la obra   *work*

la pared   *wall*

la pintura   *painting*

precolombino(a)   *pre-Columbian*

el tambor   *drum*

A. Fill in each blank in each sentence with the correct form of a **Palabra clave.**

1. Una estatua es un tipo de _____.

2. El _____ es un instrumento de percusión.

3. Generalmente usas un _____ si quieres poner una pintura en la pared.

4. El tenis y la natación son deportes que puedes practicar en un gimnasio,

   o, si hace buen tiempo, _____.

5. Las artes _____ incluyen pinturas, cerámica, esculturas y otras cosas que hicieron los indígenas.

B. Fill in each set of blanks with the correct form of a **Palabra clave.** Then unscramble the boxed letters to complete the question below.

1. En el ☐ __ __ __ __ de La Paz, hay instrumentos musicales.

2. Una ☐ __ __ __ de arte puede ser una pintura, una escultura o un mural.

3. Un museo al aire libre no tiene __ ☐ __ __ __ __ __ .

4. Si quieres ver algunas obras __ __ __ ☐ __ __ __ __ __ ☐ ☐ __ __ que hicieron los indígenas, debes ir a un museo de Latinoamérica.

5. Un mural es una __ ☐ __ ☐ __ __ __ que un artista hace en una pared.

   ¿Te gustaría visitar el __ __ __ __ __ __ __ __ __?

¿Comprendiste?

1. ¿Dónde está el Museo al Aire Libre? ¿Y el Museo de Instrumentos Musicales?

_____

_____

2. ¿Qué hay en los dos museos?

_____

_____

_____

3. ¿Por qué no es tradicional el museo de Buenos Aires? ¿Y el museo de La Paz?

_____

_____

_____

4. ¿Quiénes viven en el Caminito? ¿Cómo son sus casas?

_____

Conexión personal

Use the diagram below to reflect on a memorable museum, art exhibition, concert, movie, or play *(obra de teatro)* you have attended. In the center circle, write the name of the event or place. Then fill in the surrounding circles with the requested information.

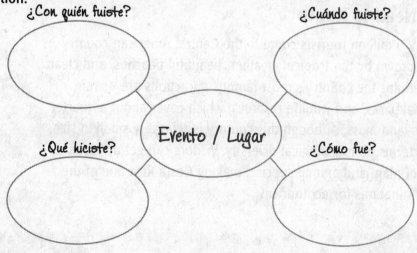

¿Con quién fuiste?

¿Cuándo fuiste?

¿Qué hiciste?

Evento / Lugar

¿Cómo fue?

Para leer   *Mi viaje a Costa Rica*

Reading Strategy

USE AN "L" TO LINK PLACE AND EVENT On the tall part of the Ls below, write the name of the place. On the low part, write the events and activities.

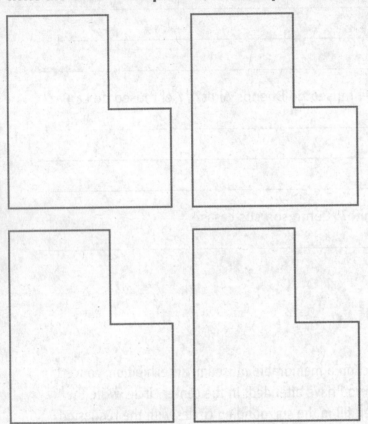

What You Need to Know

Each year, over a million tourists come to the Central American country of Costa Rica, drawn by the tropical weather, beautiful beaches, and clear waters. But perhaps the country's most famous attractions are its rain forests, national parks, and wildlife reserves, which cover about a quarter of Costa Rica's land mass. Although this country is relatively small in size, it is a giant in terms of its biological diversity. Visitors can get up close to thousands of plant and animal species, making Costa Rica one of the world's top destinations for ecotourism.

Mi viaje a Costa Rica

El año pasado Sara y su familia hicieron un viaje a Costa Rica. Cuando volvieron a Miami, Sara hizo un álbum con fotos y recuerdos de sus experiencias.

¡Papá nunca tiene miedo! Aquí está en un zip line. Aquí va de árbol en árbol en un cable de metal.

Fuimos todos al **Bosque Nuboso**[1] en Monteverde. Es una reserva biológica con muchos tipos de **árboles** y **pájaros**. Es un lugar ideal para caminar y tomar fotos.

¿Qué están mirando mi mamá y mis hermanos? No es un pájaro y no es un avión... Es papá.

Vimos un tucán. Es un pájaro bonito de muchos colores. Es típico de Costa Rica. Allí hay más de 850 **especies** de pájaros.

---
[1] cloud

PALABRAS CLAVE
el bosque *forest*
el árbol *tree*

el pájaro *bird*
la especie *species*

READING TIP This reading uses the expression **de árbol en árbol** to mean "from tree to tree." This expression is commonly used to talk about repeatedly going from one similar place to another. For example, at the mall you might go **de tienda en tienda** looking for an item.

▌MÁRCALO ◇ GRAMÁTICA

In this lesson, you learned a new tense, the present progressive. Find and circle the verb in the present progressive in the boxed text. Underline the subject of the verb.

READER'S SUCCESS STRATEGY Put a check mark next to things we know Sara and her family did in Costa Rica.

1. _____ Sara y su familia vieron pájaros.

2. _____ Sara y su familia comieron en un restaurante.

3. _____ Sara compró regalos para sus amigos.

4. _____ Sara y su familia hicieron un viaje en avión.

5. _____ Sara fue de árbol en árbol en un cable de metal.

A pensar...

What was Sara's favorite part of the trip? Why? **(Summarize)**

_____

_____

_____

_____

CHALLENGE What aspects of Sara's trip are the most interesting to you? If you had to choose three activities from her trip to do yourself, what would you choose and why? **(Connect, Evaluate)**

_____

_____

_____

_____

_____

_____

_____

_____

_____

_____

En San José, nos quedamos en un hotel en el centro. El hotel está cerca de la Plaza Central y la **Catedral** Metropolitana.

Un día fuimos a Escazú. Estoy comprando regalos para mis amigos en Miami. También compré una pequeña **máscara** de **barro**.

Hicimos un viaje en avión de San José a Tambor (en la costa del Pacífico de Costa Rica). Pasamos tres días en Montezuma. Descansamos en la playa, tomamos el sol y buceamos. ¡Fue mi parte favorita de las vacaciones!

PALABRAS CLAVE
la máscara _mask_
el barro _clay_

la catedral _cathedral_

Vocabulario de la lectura

Palabras clave

el árbol *tree*

el avión *airplane*

el barro *clay*

el bosque *forest*

la catedral *cathedral*

la especie *species*

hacer un viaje *to take a trip*

la máscara *mask*

el pájaro *bird*

quedarse en *to stay in*

A. For each **Palabra clave** in the first column, find the phrase in the second column that is closest in meaning. Write the corresponding letter in the blank.

_____ **1.** pájaro

_____ **2.** bosque

_____ **3.** especie

_____ **4.** catedral

_____ **5.** avión

a. un lugar religioso

b. un animal que va por el aire

c. una forma de transporte

d. un lugar donde hay muchos árboles

e. un tipo de animal

B. Fill in each set of blanks with the correct form of a **Palabra clave.** Then unscramble the boxed letters to complete the question below.

1. Muchas personas llevan __ __ ☐ __ __ __ __ ☐ en Halloween.

2. Cuando estoy de vacaciones, me gusta ☐☐ __ __ __ __ __ __ __ ☐ un hotel bonito.

3. El año pasado Sara __ __ __ ☐ ☐ __ __ __ __ __ __ ☐ a Costa Rica.

4. El tucán es un pájaro multicolor que vive en un __ __ ☐☐ __ .

5. El ☐ __ __ __ ☐ es un material que usamos para hacer cerámica.

¿Te gustaría ir al __ __ __ __ __ __ __ __ __ __ __ __ de Monteverde?

¿Comprendiste?

1. ¿Adónde fueron Sara y su familia en Monteverde? Si te gusta ver pájaros, ¿es Costa Rica un buen lugar? ¿Por qué?

_____

_____

2. ¿Dónde está el hotel donde se quedaron Sara y su familia?

_____

3. ¿Qué hizo Sara en Escazú?

_____

4. ¿Está Tambor cerca o lejos de San José? ¿Cómo lo sabes?

_____

_____

5. ¿Cómo es el padre de Sara?

_____

Conexión personal

Think of a trip you have taken or a trip you would like to take. Write a postcard to a friend or family member from your destination. Write your text in the right-hand side of the box, and draw a picture of an aspect of your trip in the left-hand side of the box.

	¡Hola!

Para leer *Mercados en Costa Rica y Uruguay*

Reading Strategy

DIAGRAM COMPARISONS Use a Venn diagram to compare markets and bargaining in Costa Rica, Uruguay, and the U.S.

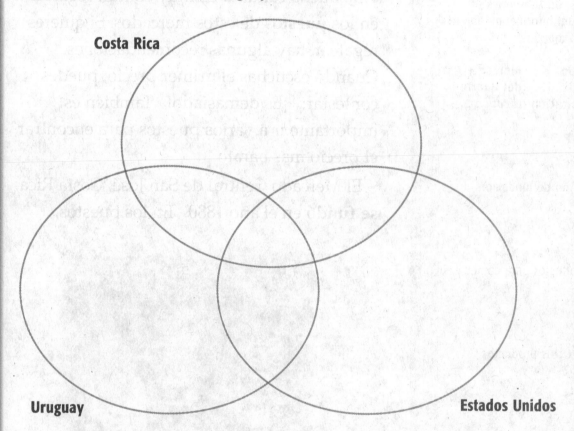

Costa Rica

Uruguay

Estados Unidos

What You Need to Know

When you are in a store and see something you like, but it's too expensive, do you look for it in another store or do you wait until it goes on sale? If you were at an outdoor market in Latin America, you would most likely bargain for a better price. In markets, bargaining is not considered out of place; on the contrary, it is expected. On the following pages, you will read about two exciting open-air markets and the items for which you might bargain while shopping there.

READING TIP Review the food vocabulary you learned in Units 3 and 4. These words, combined with the new vocabulary related to arts and handicrafts you learned in this unit, will help you understand the full range of products available at the two markets.

READER'S SUCCESS STRATEGY Use the table below to help you keep track of important information about the two markets.

Mercado Central	Mercado del Puerto
Ubicación (Location)	
Año de fundación	
Productos para comer	
Otros productos	

Mercados en Costa Rica y Uruguay 🎧

En Latinoamérica, muchas ciudades tienen mercados al aire libre, donde puedes ir de compras y encontrar artículos interesantes y de buena calidad. Es muy común regatear

5 en los **puestos** de estos mercados. Si quieres regatear, hay algunas recomendaciones. Cuando escuchas el primer precio, puedes contestar: «¡Es demasiado!» También es importante ir a varios puestos para encontrar

10 el precio más barato.

El Mercado Central de San José, Costa Rica, **se fundó** en el año 1880. En los puestos,

PALABRAS CLAVE
el puesto *stall*

fundarse *to be founded*

Mercado de fruta, Montevideo, Uruguay

venden una variedad de cosas, como café,
frutas, verduras, pescado, carne, **flores** y
15 plantas medicinales. También puedes comprar
recuerdos. Hay camisetas, joyas y artículos
de madera y de **cuero**. Si tienes hambre, hay
restaurantes pequeños que se llaman sodas.

El Mercado del Puerto está cerca del mar
20 en Montevideo, la capital de Uruguay. Se
inauguró[1] en 1868. Allí hay artistas locales
que venden sus artículos y puedes comprar
artesanías en las tiendas. También puedes
comer en los restaurantes, donde sirven
25 carne y pescado. La parrillada, un plato con
diferentes tipos de carne, es muy popular.
Los sábados, muchas
personas van a este
mercado para almorzar
30 y escuchar música.

---
[1] opened

A pensar...

Do you know of any places or
events in the U.S. that are similar to
these open-air markets? **(Connect)**

CHALLENGE Write a
conversation between yourself
and a **vendedor** *(vendor)* at the
Mercado Central in which you
bargain over the price of an item.
Be creative! *Hint:* In Costa Rica, the
prices are expressed in **colones.**
One U.S. dollar is approximately
500 colones. **(Extend)**

Yo:

Vendedor:

Yo:

Vendedor:

Yo:

Vendedor:

Yo:

MÁRCALO **GRAMÁTICA**
In this lesson, you learned
about demonstrative adjectives.
Find and underline the
demonstrative adjective in the
boxed text. Then draw two lines
under the noun it modifies.

Vocabulario de la lectura

Palabras clave

las **artesanías** *handicrafts*
los **artículos** *goods*
el **cuero** *leather*
la **flor** *flower*
fundarse *to be founded*

las **joyas** *jewelry*
el **mercado** *market*
el **puesto** *stall*
regatear *to bargain*

A. Complete each sentence with the correct form of a **Palabra clave.**

1. Las _____ incluyen cerámica y otros artículos hechos a mano *(made by hand)*.

2. Una _____ es la parte más bonita de una planta.

3. En un mercado, hay muchos _____ donde venden muchas cosas diferentes.

4. Si estás en un mercado y quieres un precio más barato,

   puedes _____.

5. En esa tienda venden muchos _____ de madera y de cuero.

B. Mark each sentence as **C** *(cierto)* or **F** *(falso).*

_____ **1.** Un mercado es un lugar donde personas vienen a vender y a comprar.

_____ **2.** Encuentras flores en un jardín.

_____ **3.** El cuero es una comida rica.

_____ **4.** Los anillos y los aretes son joyas.

_____ **5.** Si un mercado se funda, allí no venden productos.

¿Comprendiste?

1. ¿Qué puedes comprar en el Mercado Central? ¿En el Mercado del Puerto?

_____

_____

_____

2. ¿Cuál de los dos mercados es más viejo?

_____

3. ¿Qué recuerdos hay en el Mercado Central?

_____

4. ¿En qué mercado es popular la parrillada?

_____

5. ¿Por qué van muchas personas al Mercado del Puerto los sábados?

_____

Conexión personal

Which of the two markets described would you prefer to visit? Tell which market you like better and what items you would like to buy or what you would like to do there.

Me gustaría ir al...

_____

_____

_____

_____

_____

_____

_____

_____

_____

_____

_____

_____

Literatura adicional

In this section you will find literary readings in Spanish that range from poems to excerpts from novels, short stories, and other works. Each reading has biographical information about the author and background information about the selection. Like the *Lecturas culturales* readings, the literary readings have reading strategies, reading tips, reader's success strategies, critical-thinking questions, vocabulary activities, comprehension questions, and a short writing activity to help you understand each selection. There is also a **Márcalo** feature for literary analysis of the readings.

Para leer *Cumpleaños*

Reading Strategy

QUESTION Asking questions about a work of literature as you read is one way to understand the selection better. Use the five W's—who, what, where, when, why—to help you ask your questions. In the chart below, record questions and the answers you discover while reading **"Cumpleaños"** by Carmen Lomas Garza and viewing the illustration.

"Cumpleaños"

Who is the speaker?	*a young girl*
What	
Where	
When	
Why	

What You Need to Know

"Cumpleaños" is a story from Carmen Lomas Garza's book *Cuadros de familia*, in which she describes her memories of growing up in Kingsville, Texas, near the border of Mexico. Through illustrated vignettes about family activities from making tamales to picking nopal cactus, *Cuadros de familia* relates aspects of Mexican American history and culture. In **"Cumpleaños,"** Carmen Lomas Garza remembers celebrating her sixth birthday.

Sobre la autora

Carmen Lomas Garza, artista chicana, nació en Kingsville, Texas, en 1948. Empezó a estudiar arte a la edad de trece años. Sus pinturas, inspiradas en su niñez en el sur de Texas, son escenas típicas de la vida mexicano americana.

~~~~~~~~~~

Cumpleaños

Ésa soy yo, pegándole[1] a la piñata en la fiesta que me dieron cuando cumplí seis años[2]. Era[3] también el cumpleaños de mi hermano, que cumplía cuatro años. Mi madre nos dio
5 una gran fiesta e invitó a muchos primos, **vecinos** y amigos.

---

[1] hitting   [2] *cumplí seis años* I turned six   [3] It was

Cumpleaños de Lala y Tudi *by Carmen Lomas Garza, 1989*

PALABRAS CLAVE
el (la) vecino(a) *neighbor*

READING TIP Review the vocabulary you have learned for family members. Then circle the words in the story that refer to the relatives of the girl who is narrating it.

APUNTES

MÁRCALO **ANÁLISIS**
This story contains vivid descriptions, details that help the reader form a strong mental picture. Underline words or phrases in the story that help you visualize in your mind the activity and excitement of the birthday party.

READER'S SUCCESS STRATEGY As you read, look for depictions of the vocabulary in the illustration. First identify the girl who is telling the story and her father. Then find the following: **la cuerda, el palo, el pañuelo, la piñata.**

A pensar...

1. Whose birthday is it on the day of the party? **(Clarify)**

_____

_____

_____

2. What details of Mexican American culture are described in the story? **(Main Idea)**

_____

_____

_____

_____

CHALLENGE How is the birthday party described in **"Cumpleaños"** the same as or different from birthday parties you had as a child, or birthday celebrations you attended? Use the Venn diagram to record your answer. Where the circles are separate, write in differences. Where they intersect, write in similarities. **(Compare and Contrast)**

"Cumpleaños"

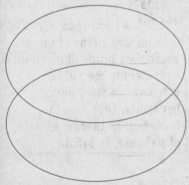

Birthdays I Remember

No puedes ver la piñata cuando le estás dando[4] con el **palo,** porque tienes los ojos cubiertos[5] por un **pañuelo.** Mi padre está

10 tirando[6] de la **cuerda** que **sube** y **baja** la piñata. Él se encargará[7] de que todos tengan[8] por lo menos una oportunidad de pegarle a la piñata. Luego alguien acabará rompiéndola[9], y entonces todos los **caramelos** que tiene

15 dentro caerán[10] y todos los niños correrán a **cogerlos.**

---

[4] **le estás dando** you're hitting it
[5] covered
[6] is pulling
[7] will make sure
[8] have
[9] **acabará rompiéndola** will end up breaking it
[10] will fall out

PALABRAS CLAVE

el palo *stick*	**bajar** *to lower*
el pañuelo *handkerchief*	**los caramelos** *candies*
la cuerda *rope*	**coger** *to grab*
subir *to raise*	

Vocabulario de la lectura

Palabras clave

bajar *to lower*	**la cuerda** *rope*	**subir** *to raise*
los caramelos *candies*	**el palo** *stick*	**el (la) vecino(a)** *neighbor*
coger *to grab*	**el pañuelo** *handkerchief*	

A. Complete the puzzle using forms of the **Palabras clave**.

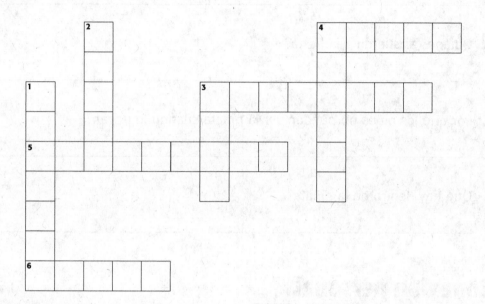

Across

3. En general son blancos.
4. Los niños corrieron a _____ los caramelos.
5. Son dulces.
6. Es lo opuesto *(opposite)* de **bajar**.

Down

1. Estas personas viven en la misma comunidad.
2. Es lo opuesto *(opposite)* de **subir**.
3. Rompes una piñata con este objeto.
4. La usas para subir y bajar la piñata.

B. Choose two **Palabras clave** and write a sentence about **"Cumpleaños"** using each one.

_____

_____

_____

_____

¿Comprendiste?

1. ¿Cuántos años tiene la narradora?

_____

2. ¿Cuántos años tiene el hermano de la narradora?

_____

3. ¿Quiénes asistieron a la fiesta?

_____

4. ¿Por qué los niños no pueden ver la piñata cuando le pegan?

_____

5. ¿Qué hay dentro de la piñata?

_____

Conexión personal

Do you have vivid recollections of any family celebrations from your childhood?
Choose a birthday, holiday, or other celebration you remember and write some
details about it in the web below.

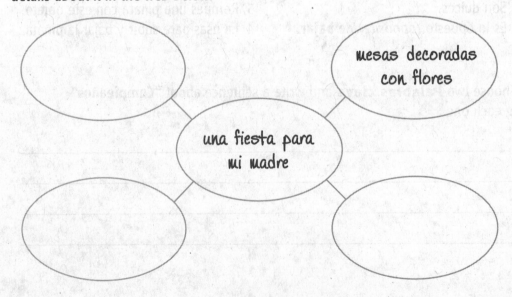

mesas decoradas
con flores

una fiesta para
mi madre

Para leer   *La exclamación / En Uxmal*

Reading Strategy

CLARIFY THE MEANING OF A POEM The process of stopping while reading to quickly review what has happened and to look for answers to questions you may have is called clarifying.
Complete the chart below by doing the following:

- Read the title and the first two lines of the poem.
- Stop to clarify those lines.
- Paraphrase what the lines are about in one of the boxes.
- Continue to read and clarify the rest of the poem in the same manner.

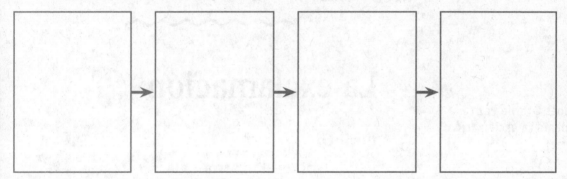

What You Need to Know

In his Nobel lecture, Octavio Paz made the following statements:

*In Mexico, the Spaniards encountered history as well as geography.
That history is still alive: It is a present rather than a past. The temples
and gods of pre-Columbian Mexico are a pile of ruins, but the spirit that
breathed life into that world has not disappeared; it speaks to us in the
hermetic language of myth, legend, forms of social coexistence, popular
art, customs. Being a Mexican writer means listening to the voice of that
present, that presence.*

. . . .

*Poetry is in love with the instant and seeks to relive it in the poem, thus
separating it from sequential time and turning it into a fixed present.*

Consider how these ideas are reflected in the poems that follow.

READER'S SUCCESS STRATEGY Don't worry if you can't understand the poems all at once. Focus on what you do understand, and build from that.

A pensar...

1. Form is the placement of a poem's lines on the page. What is the significance of the way the lines are staggered on the page in **"La exclamación"**? (Draw Conclusions)

2. Why does Octavio Paz call this poem **"La exclamación"**? (Analyze)

MÁRCALO ANÁLISIS
Repetition is a literary technique in which sounds, words, phrases, or lines are repeated for emphasis. Reread **"La exclamación"** and circle each phrase that appears more than once. Why do you think the poet repeats these phrases one after the other?

Sobre el autor

Octavio Paz (1914–1998), poeta y ensayista que ganó el Premio Nobel de Literatura en 1990, nació en la Ciudad de México. Durante los años cincuenta publicó *El laberinto de soledad (The Labyrinth of Solitude),* una colección de ensayos sobre la identidad mexicana, y *Libertad bajo palabra (Liberty Under Oath),* que contiene el poema «Piedra de sol» («Sunstone»). Inspirado en el calendario azteca, «Piedra de sol» es tal vez su obra más famosa. Desde 1962 hasta 1968 Octavio Paz fue embajador de México en India. Vivió en varios países y su escritura refleja una perspectiva internacional. Paz escribió sobre muchos temas, incluso sobre política, filosofía y amor.

La exclamación

Quieto
> no en la **rama**
en el aire
> No en el aire
5   en el instante
> el **colibrí**

PALABRAS CLAVE
quieto(a) *still, motionless*   **el colibrí** *hummingbird*
la rama *branch*

READING TIP Uxmal, located on the Yucatan Peninsula in Mexico, is the site of an ancient Mayan civilization.

▯▯▯ MÁRCALO ◇ **ANÁLISIS**
Personification is a figure of speech that gives human characteristics to an object, animal, or idea. Circle the line containing personification in **"En Uxmal."** What is being personified?

_____

_____

A pensar...

1. Consider that this poem was inspired by the ruins of an ancient civilization. What do you think the poet means when he says a bird has stopped in the air? (**Analyze**)

_____

_____

2. What does the poet mean when he says time is transparent? (**Analyze**)

_____

_____

CHALLENGE How are these two poems similar? How are they different? (**Compare and Contrast**)

_____

_____

En Uxmal 🎧

Mediodía

La **luz** no **parpadea,**
el tiempo se vacía[1] de minutos,
se ha detenido[2] un pájaro en el aire.

5 *Pleno*[3] *sol*

La hora es transparente:
vemos, si es invisible el pájaro,
el color de su **canto.**

---
[1] empties itself   [2] has stopped   [3] full

PALABRAS CLAVE
la luz   *light*
parpadear   *to blink*

el canto   *song*

Vocabulario de la lectura

Palabras clave

el canto *song*   **la luz** *light*   **quieto(a)** *still, motionless*
el colibrí *hummingbird*   **parpadear** *to blink*   **la rama** *branch*

A. Complete each analogy with one of the **Palabras clave.** In an analogy, the last two words must be related in the same way that the first two are related.

1. CABEZA : PELO : : árbol : _____

2. LEER : LIBRO : : cantar : _____

3. PUERTA : CERRAR : : ojo : _____

4. BEBIDA : REFRESCO : : pájaro : _____

5. FELIZ : ALEGRE : : tranquilo : _____

B. Complete each sentence with the correct form of a **Palabra clave.**

1. El _____ puede moverse con extraordinaria rapidez.

2. Apaga la _____, por favor; quiero dormir.

3. Hay un pájaro raro sobre la _____ de ese árbol.

4. No veo el pájaro, pero oigo su _____.

5. _____ significa «cerrar y abrir los ojos».

¿Comprendiste?

1. ¿Qué tipo de pájaro se describe en **«La exclamación»**?

_____

2. ¿En qué tres lugares se encuentra el colibrí?

_____

3. ¿A qué hora empieza el primer verso de **«En Uxmal»**?

_____

4. ¿En el segundo verso de **«En Uxmal»**, ¿qué palabra usa el poeta para describir la hora?

_____

5. ¿Qué palabra usa el poeta para describir el pájaro de **«En Uxmal»**? Si el pájaro es invisible, ¿cómo sabemos que existe?

_____

Conexión personal

If you were a poet, what would you write about? Would it be something in nature, a place you have been, or another subject? In the center of the web write a subject for your poem. Then brainstorm words you associate with it.

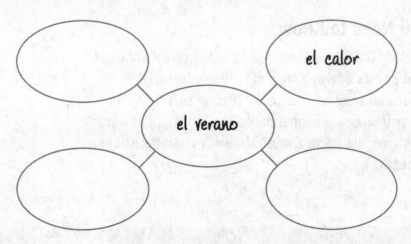

Para leer   *Palma sola*

Reading Strategy

SETTING The setting of a poem or story is the time and place where the action occurs. The setting may be a backdrop, with no effect on what happens, or it may be important to the meaning of the poem. Use the chart below to jot down lines from **"Palma sola"** that indicate setting.

Time/Place	Meaning
bajo la luna y el sol	shows the passage of time

What You Need to Know

Many of Nicolás Guillén's poems belong to the Afro-Caribbean genre called **poesía negra,** a style of writing influenced by traditional African song and dance. In **"Palma sola,"** Guillén describes a palm tree alone on a patio. The repetition of words and phrases gives the poem a musical quality characteristic of **poesía negra**.

Sobre el autor

El Poeta Nacional de Cuba, Nicolás Guillén (1902–1989) es uno de los escritores latinos más conocidos. Su poesía celebra la herencia africana de la gente cubana y la historia étnica de la isla. Guillén admiró la literatura española y la poesía clásica española. Sus poemas combinan elementos de la poesía española con el lenguaje común de los cubanos. En muchas de sus obras se puede ver el ritmo de *son,* un tipo de música de origen africano y español.

Palma sola

La palma que está en el patio
nació[1] sola;
creció sin que yo la viera[2],
creció sola;
5 **bajo** la **luna** y el sol,
vive sola.

Con su largo cuerpo fijo[3],
palma sola;
sola en el patio sellado[4],
10 siempre sola,
guardián[5] del atardecer[6],
sueña[7] sola.

---

[1] was born   [2] **sin que yo la viera** without my seeing it
[3] fixed, stationary   [4] sealed, enclosed   [5] watchman
[6] late afternoon   [7] dreams

PALABRAS CLAVE
crecer *to grow*   **la luna** *moon*
bajo *under*

READING TIP Poetry is like words and music all rolled up into one package. Rhythm, the pattern of heavy and light stresses, is one way poets add this musical quality. As you read **"Palma sola,"** notice how Guillén repeats certain words to give the poem rhythm.

MÁRCALO ANÁLISIS
Remember that **personification** is a literary device that gives human characteristics to something nonhuman. Circle the lines in this poem containing personification.

A pensar…

1. What phrases does the poet use to describe the solitary existence of the palm? **(Clarify)**

2. How is the palm tree in the poem different from a palm tree found in nature? **(Compare and Contrast)**

3. Why do you think the poet repeats the words **palma** and **sola** throughout the poem? **(Analyze)**

La palma sola **soñando,**

palma sola,

15 que va **libre** por[8] el viento,

libre y sola,

suelta[9] de **raíz** y **tierra,**

suelta y sola;

cazadora[10] de las nubes,

20 palma sola,

palma sola,

palma.

_____

[8] through   [9] free   [10] huntress

PALABRAS CLAVE

soñar   *to dream*   **el raíz (pl. raíces)**   *root*
libre   *free*   **la tierra**   *earth, soil*

Vocabulario de la lectura

Palabras clave

bajo *under*   **la luna** *moon*   **soñar** *to dream*

crecer *to grow*   **el raíz** (pl. **raíces**) *root*   **la tierra** *earth, soil*

libre *free*

A. Complete the puzzle using forms of the **Palabras clave.**

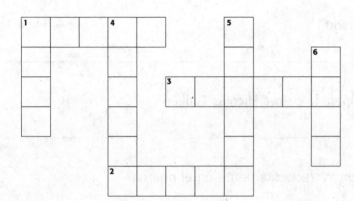

Across

1. ¿Qué haces en tu tiempo _____?
2. Lo haces cuando estás durmiendo.
3. La palma del poema es «suelta de raíz
   y _____».

Down

1. La ves por la noche.
4. Los árboles y las plantas los tienen.
5. Es el proceso de hacerse más grande.
6. Es lo opuesto *(opposite)* de **encima**.

B. Choose three of the **Palabras clave** and write a sentence with each one.

_____

_____

_____

_____

_____

_____

_____

¿Comprendiste?

1. ¿Qué es una palma?

_____

2. ¿Dónde está la palma del poema?

_____

3. ¿Es el patio abierto o sellado?

_____

4. ¿Con qué dos cosas compara la palma Nicolás Guillén?

_____

5. ¿Qué dos palabras se repiten frecuentemente en el poema?

_____

Conexión personal

Nicolás Guillén chose a palm tree on a patio to represent the concept of solitude **(la soledad)**. If you were a poet, what things would you use to illustrate the state of being alone? Use the word web to jot down your ideas. Some words have been provided as examples.

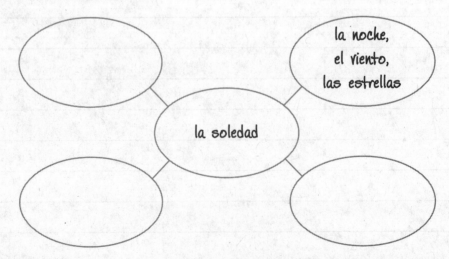

la noche, el viento, las estrellas

la soledad

Para leer   *Como agua para chocolate*

Reading Strategy

CONNECT TO YOUR OWN LIFE You can connect the subject
of a reading to your own life. As you read the recipe from
Como agua para chocolate, think about foods and recipes that
have special meaning for you. Compare Laura Esquivel's recipe
for making chocolate to one of your own recipes.

Chocolate	My Recipe
only two ingredients	lots of ingredients

What You Need to Know

This reading is a recipe from the novel *Como agua para chocolate*
by Mexican writer Laura Esquivel. The book is in the form of monthly
installments with food and home remedies used to describe the life and
loves of the main character. The recipe is for chocolate, which is made
from the seeds, or beans, of the cacao tree. The word **cacao** is Spanish,
from the Nahuatl word *cacahuatl*. Cacao was so prized by the Aztecs that
the beans were used as a form of currency. The Aztecs also ground the
beans to produce a rich chocolate beverage.

READING TIP Remember the food and cooking vocabulary you have learned: **libras, azúcar, aceite, caliente, cuchillo.** You can figure out new words like **tostar** and **granos** because they are cognates.

☰ **MÁRCALO** ⬦ **ANÁLISIS** This reading contains **sensory details,** descriptive words that have to do with the senses. Reread the recipe and highlight phrases or passages that have to do with sight, taste, and touch. Then write them in the appropriate category in the chart below.

la vista *(sight)*	
el gusto *(taste)*	
el tacto *(touch)*	

APUNTES

_____

_____

_____

_____

_____

_____

_____

_____

_____

Sobre la autora

Laura Esquivel nació en México en 1950. Empezó su carrera de escritora como guionista *(scriptwriter)* de películas. En 1989 publicó la novela *Como agua para chocolate,* que ganó mucha popularidad tanto en Latinoamérica como en Estados Unidos. En 1992, la película basada en la novela tuvo mucho éxito y Esquivel ganó el premio Ariel (de la Academia Mexicana de Ciencias y Artes Cinematográficas) al mejor guión.

〜〜〜〜〜〜〜〜〜〜

Como agua para chocolate

Ingredientes chocolate:

2 libras Cacao Soconusco

2 libras Cacao Maracaibo

2 libras Cacao Caracas

Azúcar entre 4 y 6 libras según el gusto

Manera de hacerse:

La primera operación es tostar el cacao. Para hacerlo es conveniente utilizar una charola de hojalata[1] en vez del comal[2], pues el aceite que se desprende[3] de los granos se pierde entre
5 los poros del comal. Es importantísimo poner cuidado en este tipo de indicaciones, pues la **bondad** del chocolate depende de tres cosas, a saber: de que el cacao que se emplee esté sano[4] y no averiado[5], de que se mezclen[6] en
10 su **fabricación** distintas clases de cacao y, por último, de su **grado** de tueste[7].

El grado de tueste **aconsejable** es el del momento en que el cacao comienza a despedir[8] su aceite. Si se retira[9] antes, aparte de presentar
15 un **aspecto** descolorido y **desagradable,** lo hará indigesto[10]. Por el contrario, si se deja más tiempo sobre el fuego[11], el grano quedará **quemado** en gran parte y contaminará de acrimonia y aspereza al chocolate[12].

(…)

---

[1] **charola de hojalata** pan made of tin   [2] clay griddle
[3] is given off   [4] in good condition; intact
[5] damaged; spoiled   [6] are mixed
[7] toasting
[8] **comienza a despedir** starts to give off
[9] it is removed
[10] it will be indigestible
[11] flame, heat
[12] **contaminará de acrimonia y aspereza** will make bitter and acrid

READER'S SUCCESS STRATEGY As you read, make a list below of the kitchen equipment used in the recipe. Then write the verb from the recipe that indicates what each item is used to do.

APUNTES

CHALLENGE Do you think that it would be easy or difficult to use this recipe? Why? **(Evaluate)**

PALABRAS CLAVE
la bondad *goodness*   **el aspecto** *appearance, aspect*
la fabricación *making, manufacture*   **desagradable** *disagreeable, unpleasant*
el grado *degree*   **quemado(a)** *burned*
aconsejable *advisable*

A pensar...

1. Write the numbers 1, 2, 3, 4, or 5 to show the order of steps in the recipe. **(Chronological Order)**

____ Divide the mass into chunks.

____ Separate the hulls with a sieve.

____ Add the sugar and pound the mixture.

____ Toast the beans in a pan made of tin.

____ Grind the beans on a metate.

2. What three things does the goodness of the chocolate depend on? Circle the correct answers. **(Identify Main Idea and Details)**

the bitterness of the cacao beans

the mixing of different kinds of beans

the undamaged condition of the beans

the use of a clay griddle to toast the beans

the degree of toasting of the beans

3. What happens when the cacao is not toasted enough and when it is toasted too much? **(Cause and Effect)**

_____

_____

_____

_____

_____

20 Cuando el cacao ya está tostado como se indicó, se limpia utilizando un cedazo[13] para separar la cáscara[14] del grano. Debajo del metate[15] donde se ha de **moler**[16], se pone un cajete[17] con buena lumbre[18] y cuando ya

25 está caliente el metate, se procede a moler el grano. Se mezcla entonces con el azúcar, **machacándolo** con un mazo[19] y moliendo las dos cosas juntas. En seguida se divide la masa en **trozos.** Con las manos se moldean

30 las tablillas[20], redondas o alargadas[21], según el gusto, y se ponen a orear[22]. Con la punta[23] de un cuchillo se le pueden señalar[24] las divisiones que se deseen[25].

---

[13] sieve   [14] hull   [15] grinding stone
[16] **se ha de moler** it is to be ground   [17] earthenware bowl
[18] hot fire   [19] mallet, wooden hammer   [20] tablets
[21] round or elongated   [22] to air   [23] tip
[24] to mark   [25] are desired

PALABRAS CLAVE

moler *to grind*   **el trozo** *chunk, piece*
machacar *to pound*

Vocabulario de la lectura

Palabras clave

aconsejable *advisable*	**el grado** *degree*
el aspecto *appearance, aspect*	**machacar** *to pound*
la bondad *goodness*	**moler** *to grind*
desagradable *disagreeable, unpleasant*	**quemado(a)** *burned*
la fabricación *making, manufacture*	**el trozo** *chunk, piece*

A. Complete each sentence with a **Palabra clave.**

1. El _____ de tueste es el del momento en que el cacao empieza a despedir su aceite.

2. El cacao presenta un _____ descolorido si se retira antes.

3. Si se deja más tiempo sobre el fuego, el grano queda _____.

4. Se procede a _____ el grano con un metate.

5. Hay que _____ el grano y el azúcar con un mazo.

B. On the blank line next to each group of words, write the **Palabra clave** that goes with each set of clues.

1. cualidad; bueno _____

2. hacer; productos, comida _____

3. fragmento, porción, pedazo _____

4. feo, horrible _____

5. recomendable, apropiado _____

¿Comprendiste?

1. ¿Cuántas libras de cacao necesitas para preparar la receta?

_____

2. ¿Cuál es el otro ingrediente?

_____

3. ¿Qué haces primero?

_____

4. ¿Cuándo procedes a moler el grano?

_____

5. ¿Cómo se moldea las tablillas?

_____

Conexión personal

Do you like chocolate? What other foods do you like? List them in the chart and write a couple of adjectives to describe each one.

Comida	Descripción
chocolate	dulce, marrón

Para leer *Don Quijote de la Mancha*

Reading Strategy

UNDERSTAND CHARACTER'S MOTIVES Motives are the emotions, wants, or needs that cause a character to act or react in a certain way. As you read this retelling of the beginning of *Don Quijote de la Mancha,* use the chart below to understand the actions of don Quijote. Next to each action, describe the reason, or motivation, he had for taking it.

Action	Reason
1. He wants to travel the world in search of adventure.	He wants to be like the knight-errant heroes in books of chivalry.
2. He adds his region's name, *la Mancha,* to his own name.	
3. He polishes the armor that belonged to his great-grandfather.	
4. He names his horse Rocinante.	
5. He imagines that Aldonza Lorenzo is a noble lady.	

What You Need to Know

The following selection is an adaptation of the first chapter of *El ingenioso hidalgo don Quijote de la Mancha,* the famous novel by Miguel de Cervantes. Romances of chivalry, the books that "dried out" don Quijote's brain, were popular reading between the Middle Ages and the Renaissance. Knight-errants, frequent heroes in books of chivalry, wandered in search of adventure to prove their bravery, honor, and gallantry toward women.

APUNTES

Sobre el autor

Miguel de Cervantes Saavedra (1547–1616) nació en Alcalá de Henares, España. Fue soldado y luchó en Lepanto, donde perdió el uso de la mano izquierda. Más tarde fue capturado por piratas y pasó cinco años prisionero. Escribió en todos los géneros. Algunas de sus obras son *Viaje del Parnaso* (poesía); *Comedias y entremeses* (drama); y su obra más famosa, *Don Quijote de la Mancha,* que se publicó en dos partes y puede ser la novela más importante de la literatura universal. Aunque *Don Quijote* fue un éxito inmediato, Cervantes fue pobre toda la vida.

El famoso hidalgo don Quijote de la Mancha

Había una vez[1] un **hidalgo pobre** en un lugar de España que se llama la Mancha. En su casa había[2] muchísimos libros de **caballería** porque el pasatiempo favorito de
5 este señor era[3] leer y leer, especialmente libros de caballería. Se pasaba[4] las noches completas sin dormir, leyendo hasta el **amanecer,** y lo mismo durante el día.

---

[1] **Había una vez** Once upon a time there was   [2] there were
[3] was   [4] He spent

PALABRAS CLAVE

el (la) hidalgo(a) *person of noble descent*	la caballería *chivalry*
pobre *poor*	el amanecer *dawn*

Leyó tantos y tantos libros que un día <u>se</u>
10 <u>le secó el **cerebro**</u>[5] y perdió el juicio[6]. Se
imaginó todo tipo de situaciones: batallas,
desafíos[7], encantamientos[8], heridas[9], **amores,**
tormentas[10] y muchas otras cosas imposibles.
Para él todas estas cosas eran[11] reales, tan
15 reales como su casa, el ama[12] de cuarenta
años, su sobrina de diecinueve años, su **rocín**
flaco y el mozo[13].

Un día resuelve **hacerse caballero andante.**
Decide ir por todo el mundo con sus armas y
20 caballo a buscar aventuras. Desea pelear[14] por
la justicia como los caballeros andantes de las
novelas que le gustan. Se va por el mundo a
buscar honra y fama.

Primero limpia las armas que fueron de su
25 **bisabuelo.** Después decide que el rocín de un
caballero andante tiene que tener un nombre
impresionante. «Rocinante te voy a llamar»,
le dice a su rocín. Luego cambia su propio[15]
nombre para incorporar el nombre de su
30 región y hacerla famosa. De esa forma se
convierte en[16] don Quijote de la Mancha.

---

[5] **se le secó el cerebro** his brain dried out [6] sanity [7] duels
[8] enchantments [9] injuries [10] misfortunes [11] were
[12] housekeeper [13] stable boy [14] to fight [15] own
[16] **se convierte en** he becomes

PALABRAS CLAVE
el cerebro brain
los amores love affairs
el rocín workhorse
flaco(a) thin

hacerse to become
el caballero andante knight-errant
el bisabuelo great-grandfather

READING TIP This reading
contains several plays on
words. **Quijote**, the name of
the central character, is also
the word for a piece of armor.
Rocinante is made up of two
words: **rocín** (workhorse),
and **ante** (before). **Dulcinea**,
the name of Quijote's lady, is
inspired by the word **dulce**.

📖 **MÁRCALO** ⟫ **ANÁLISIS**
Hyperbole is a figure of speech
in which exaggeration is used
for emphasis or effect, as in
This book weighs a ton. Find
and underline an example
of hyperbole in the second
paragraph of this reading.

APUNTES

A pensar...

1. Write the numbers 1, 2, 3, and 4 to show the order in which don Quijote does the following things. (**Chronological Order**)

_____ He names his horse *Rocinante*.

_____ He decides to call Aldonza Lorenzo *Dulcinea del Toboso*.

_____ He changes his own name to *don Quijote de la Mancha*.

_____ He polishes the armor that belonged to his great-grandfather.

2. Why does don Quijote want to become a knight-errant? (**Clarify**)

_____

_____

_____

_____

CHALLENGE What does Cervantes suggest about books of chivalry? What evidence can you find in the reading to support your answer? (**Infer**)

_____

_____

_____

_____

_____

_____

_____

Por último, como buen caballero andante, necesita una enamorada[17] a quien dedicarle sus grandes **hazañas.** En Toboso, un lugar

35 cerca de la Mancha, hay una moza labradora[18], Aldonza Lorenzo, de la que antes estuvo **enamorado.** En su imaginación Aldonza se convierte en la **dama** de sus **sueños.** Es así como nace la figura de Dulcinea del Toboso,

40 porque así se llama el lugar donde ella vive.

[17] girlfriend [18] **moza labradora** peasant girl

PALABRAS CLAVE
la hazaña *feat; heroic deed* **la dama** *lady*
enamorado(a) (de) *in love (with)* **el sueño** *dream*

Vocabulario de la lectura

Palabras clave

el amanecer *dawn*
los amores *love affairs*
el bisabuelo *great-grandfather*
la caballería *chivalry*
el caballero andante *knight-errant*
el cerebro *brain*
la dama *lady*
enamorado(a) (de) *in love (with)*

flaco(a) *thin*
hacerse *to become*
la hazaña *feat; heroic deed*
el (la) hidalgo(a) *person of noble descent*
pobre *poor*
el rocín *workhorse*
el sueño *dream*

A. Complete each analogy with one of the **Palabras clave.** In an analogy, the last two words must be related in the same way that the first two are related.

1. CAMINAR : PIERNAS : : pensar : _____

2. PÁJARO: LORO : : caballo : _____

3. ALTO : BAJO : : gordo : _____

4. HIJO: PADRE : : abuelo : _____

5. MIRAR: VER : : fantasía : _____

B. Complete each sentence with the correct form of a **Palabra clave.**

Don Quijote es un _____ que vive en la Mancha. Tiene pocas
                         (1)

posesiones; es _____. También está loco a causa de leer tantos
                    (2)

libros de _____. Pasa muchas noches sin dormir, leyendo estos
               (3)

libros hasta el _____. Un día, decide hacerse _____
                     (4)   (5)

que se va por el mundo a buscar honra y fama. Primero, limpia las armas de

su _____. Luego, cambia el nombre de su _____ a
       (6)   (7)

Rocinante. Por último, imagina que Aldonza Lorenzo, una moza labradora, es la

_____ de sus sueños y la llama Dulcinea del Toboso.
       (8)

¿Comprendiste?

1. ¿Quién es don Quijote?

_____

2. ¿Qué tipo de libros le gusta leer?

_____

3. ¿Por qué se le secó el cerebro?

_____

4. ¿Qué resuelve hacerse don Quijote?

_____

5. ¿Cómo se llama su caballo?

_____

6. ¿Quién es Aldonza Lorenzo? ¿Qué nombre le da don Quijote?

_____

Conexión personal

Many adventure stories involve a quest, a journey that a character makes to reach a certain goal. Think of characters in books, movies, or television shows that go on quests. List them in the chart below.

Personaje (Character)	De	Meta (Goal)
don Quijote	Don Quijote de la Mancha	pelear por la justicia

Para leer   *Oda al tomate*

Reading Strategy

WORD CHOICE Writers choose their words with care in order to express their thoughts accurately. Through careful word choice, a writer can make readers feel a certain way or visualize an image. As you read "Oda al tomate," think about how certain words and phrases affect you as a reader. Use the chart below to record interesting words and phrases and what they convey to you.

Words and Phrases	Ideas and Feelings They Convey
"el tomate invade las cocinas"	expresses the abundance of tomatoes
"su color fogoso"	conveys an image of their bright red color

What You Need to Know

This reading is the poem **"Oda al tomate"** from the book *Odas elementales* (1954) by the Chilean poet Pablo Neruda (1904–1973). Odes are long lyric poems, usually of a serious or meditative nature and having an elevated style and formal structure. Unlike most odes, those of Pablo Neruda exalt the ordinary and the everyday, from tomatoes and artichokes to the air and rain.

READING TIP Read the poem aloud. Let punctuation show you where to stop or pause. How many sentences are there in the poem? A capital letter begins each one. Write your answer on the line below.

APUNTES

_____

_____

_____

_____

_____

_____

_____

|||MÁRCALO ⟩ **ANÁLISIS**
Remember that **personification** is the attribution of human characteristics to an object, animal, or idea. Pablo Neruda uses personification to give life to foods. Find and circle examples of personification in the poem. Which foods are personified? Write your answer on the lines below.

_____

_____

_____

CHALLENGE Why would the street be filled with tomatoes? **(Draw Conclusions)**

_____

_____

_____

Sobre el autor

Pablo Neruda nació en Parral, Chile. Su verdadero nombre era Ricardo Neftalí Reyes. Estudió pedagogía en francés en la Universidad de Chile. Allí conoció a Albertina Azócar. A ella le dedica los primeros poemas de _Veinte poemas de amor y una canción desesperada_ (1924). Para Neruda, todo puede ser poesía. En sus famosas _Odas elementales_ escribió versos para el tomate, el átomo, un reloj, la pobreza y la soledad. Pablo Neruda fue diplomático en varios países de Europa y en México. En 1971 obtuvo el Premio Nobel de Literatura.

〜〜〜〜〜〜〜

Oda al tomate

La calle
se **llenó** de tomates,
mediodía,
verano,
5 la luz
se parte[1]
en dos
mitades
de tomate,
10 corre
por las calles
el jugo.

[1] is split

PALABRAS CLAVE
llenar _to fill_   la mitad _half_

En diciembre
se desata[2]

15 el tomate,
invade
las cocinas,
entra por los almuerzos,
se sienta[3]

20 reposado[4]
en los aparadores[5],
entre los vasos,
las mantequilleras[6],
los saleros[7] azules.

25 Tiene
luz propia,
majestad benigna.
Debemos, por desgracia[8],
asesinarlo:

30 se hunde[9]
el cuchillo
en su pulpa **viviente,**
en una roja
víscera,

35 un sol
fresco,
profundo,

---

[2] breaks loose   [3] sits down   [4] relaxed
[5] sideboards   [6] butter dishes [7] saltcellars
[8] unfortunately   [9] sinks

APUNTES

CHALLENGE Why is it
December and yet it is
summertime in the poem?
(Evaluate)

PALABRAS CLAVE
viviente *living*

A pensar...

1. Why do you think the poet compares the tomato to the sun? **(Draw Conclusions)**

2. What do you think the phrase **la cintura del verano** means? **(Analyze)**

APUNTES

inagotable[10],

llena de ensaladas

40 de Chile,

se casa[11] alegremente

con la clara cebolla,

y para celebrarlo

se deja

45 caer[12]

aceite,

hijo

esencial del olivo,

sobre sus hemisferios entreabiertos[13],

50 **agrega**

la pimienta

su fragancia,

la sal su magnetismo:

son las bodas[14]

55 del día,

el perejil

levanta

banderines[15],

las papas

60 hierven[16] vigorosamente,

el **asado**

golpea[17]

---

[10] inexhaustible   [11] it marries
[12] **se deja caer** is dropped   [13] halved
[14] weddings
[15] **perejil levanta banderines** parsley hoists its flag
[16] boil, bubble   [17] beats

PALABRAS CLAVE
  agregar *to add*   **el asado** *roasted meat*

con su aroma
en la puerta,
65 es hora!
vamos!
y sobre
la mesa, en la **cintura**
del verano,
70 el tomate,
astro[18] de tierra,
estrella
repetida
y **fecunda,**
75 nos muestra[19]
sus circunvoluciones[20],
sus canales,
la insigne plenitud[21]
y la abundancia
80 sin hueso[22],
sin coraza[23],
sin escamas[24] ni **espinas,**
nos entrega[25]
el regalo
85 de su color **fogoso**
y la totalidad de su **frescura.**

[18] star   [19] shows   [20] convolutions, folds
[21] celebrated fullness   [22] stone, pit
[23] shell   [24] scales   [25] delivers

MÁRCALO ANÁLISIS
Parallelism is a literary device in which related ideas are phrased in similar ways. An example is *a time to laugh, a time to weep*. Find and underline an example of parallelism near the end of the poem. What word is used in each line? Write the word on the line below.

_____

_____

APUNTES

PALABRAS CLAVE
   la cintura   *waist, waistline*   **fogoso(a)** *fiery*
   fecundo(a) *fertile*   **la frescura** *freshness, coolness*
   la espina *thorn*

Vocabulario de la lectura

Palabras clave

agregar *to add*	**fecundo(a)** *fertile*	**llenar** *to fill*
el asado *roasted meat*	**fogoso(a)** *fiery*	**la mitad** *half*
la cintura *waist, waistline*	**la frescura** *freshness, coolness*	**viviente** *living*
la espina *thorn*		

A. On the line next to each word pair, write whether the words are synonyms or antonyms. Synonyms are words with the same or similar meaning. Antonyms are words with opposite meanings.

1. calor–frescura _____

2. adicionar–agregar _____

3. fértil–fecundo _____

4. ardiente–fogoso _____

B. Answer each question by writing one of the **Palabras clave** in the blank.

1. ¿Qué palabra es un tipo de preparación de carne? _____

2. ¿Qué palabra significa algo que vive? _____

3. ¿Qué haces con un vaso? _____

4. ¿Qué palabra es una parte del cuerpo humano? _____

5. ¿Qué tiene una rosa? _____

6. ¿Qué palabra significa «una de dos partes»? _____

¿Comprendiste?

1. ¿En qué mes ocurre el poema?

_____

2. ¿Qué tiene el tomate?

_____

3. ¿Qué no tiene el tomate?

_____

4. ¿Cuáles son los ingredientes de la ensalada?

_____

Conexión personal

Of the ordinary and the everyday, what would you write an ode to? Decide on a subject for your ode and write a list of words and phrases you would use to describe it in the notebook at the right. Include at least one example of personification.

Oda a _____

_____

_____

_____

_____

_____

_____

_____

_____

_____

_____

_____

Academic and Informational Reading

In this section you'll find strategies to help you read all kinds of informational materials. The examples here range from magazines you read for fun to textbooks to bus schedules. Applying these simple and effective techniques will help you be a successful reader of the many texts you encounter every day.

Reading a Magazine Article

A magazine article is designed to catch and hold your interest. You will get the most from your reading if you recognize the special features of a magazine page and learn how to use them. Look at the sample magazine article as you read each strategy below.

A Read the **title** to get an idea of what the article is about. Scan any other **headings** to see how information in the article is organized.

B As you read, notice any **quotations.** Who is quoted? Is the person a reliable source on the subject?

C Notice information set in special type, such as **italics** or **boldface.** For example, look at the caption in the article that is set in italic type.

D Study **visuals,** such as charts, graphs, pictures, maps, and bulleted lists. Visuals add important information and bring the topic to life.

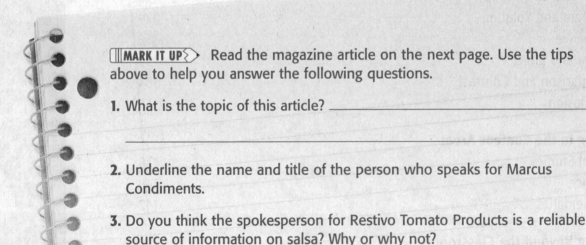

MARK IT UP Read the magazine article on the next page. Use the tips above to help you answer the following questions.

1. What is the topic of this article? _____

_____

2. Underline the name and title of the person who speaks for Marcus Condiments.

3. Do you think the spokesperson for Restivo Tomato Products is a reliable source of information on salsa? Why or why not?

_____

_____

4. Circle the caption set in italic type.

5. Draw a box around the visual that compares the sales of ketchup and salsa.

A SALSA AND KETCHUP BATTLE IT OUT FOR TOP SAUCE

When you want to add a little spice to your snack or supper, do you reach for the salsa or the ketchup? Until recently, sales figures showed that more people grabbed the ketchup bottle, slathering the tomato sauce on their hamburgers, hot dogs, French fries, mashed potatoes, scrambled eggs, green beans, and almost anything else you can imagine. Elvis Presley even used it as a topping for sweet potato pie.

In 1996, however, salsa moved into number one position, replacing ketchup as the nation's top tomato sauce. Since then, the two condiments have been battling it out, with ketchup frantically trying to play catch-up. And it seems to have **B** succeeded. "Salsa's popularity has peaked. Ketchup is back on top," boasts Peter Harrington, chief executive of the world's largest ketchup maker, Marcus Condiments.

Salsa producers do not seem overly concerned, though. Mary Sullivan, a senior marketing manager for a leading salsa maker, Restivo Tomato Products, confidently noted that salsa is perfectly able to keep pace with ketchup. It's every bit as versatile a sauce, she says. "We're not limited to hamburgers and hot dogs." Every day, more people spoon more salsa over a whole alphabet of foods, from avocados to ziti.

To increase their slim lead over salsa, Marcus Condiments is focusing on research that shows families with children use three times more ketchup than childless households.

The salsa-ketchup war probably will not be decided any time soon. And maybe it shouldn't be. After all, to update an old saying, "Variety is the spice of life"—and of tomato sauce, too.

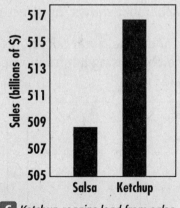

D

C *Ketchup regains lead from salsa.*

Reading a Textbook

The first page of a textbook lesson introduces you to a particular topic. The page also provides important information that will guide you through the rest of the lesson. Look at the sample textbook page as you read each strategy below.

A Preview the **title** and other **headings** to find out the lesson's main topic and related subtopics.

B Read the **key ideas** or **objectives** at the top of the page. Keep these in mind as you read. They will help you set a purpose for your reading.

C Look for a list of terms or **vocabulary words** at the start of each lesson. These words will be identified and defined throughout the lesson.

D Study **visuals** such as photographs and illustrations. Read the **captions.** Visuals can add information and interest to the topic.

IIIMARK IT UP Read the sample textbook page. Then use the strategies above to help you answer the following questions.

1. What is the topic of this lesson? _____

_____

2. Circle the key idea of the lesson.

3. Draw a box around the vocabulary words that will be defined in the lesson.

4. Put a star next to the visual that shows the structure of a sea arch.

5. Using a graphic organizer can help you take notes on the textbook material you learn. Complete the chart using information on shoreline features from the lesson.

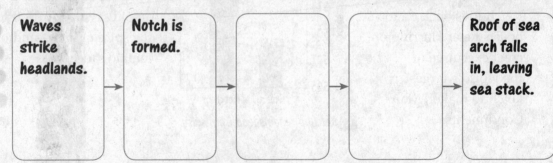

| Waves strike headlands. | → | Notch is formed. | → | | → | | → | Roof of sea arch falls in, leaving sea stack. |

A Shoreline Features

Ocean waves change the shape of a shoreline by eroding rock materials and by depositing sediments.

Waves and Erosion

Breaking storm waves may strike rock cliffs with a force of thousands of kilograms per square meter. Such breakers easily remove large masses of loose sand and clay. Air and water driven into cracks and fissures may split bedrock apart. Sand and pebbles carried by the water abrade the bedrock. Waves pound loose rock and boulders into pebbles and sand. In addition, seawater dissolves minerals from rocks such as limestone.

When waves strike the headlands of a deep-water shoreline, they may cut away the rock up to the high-tide level, forming a notch. If the materials overhanging the notch collapse, a sea cliff results.

Cliffs made of soft materials such as soil and sand wear away very quickly. For example, waves washing up on Cape Cod in Massachusetts are carrying away materials from sand cliffs there so rapidly that the cliffs are receding at a rate of about one meter every year.

In cliffs made of harder rock materials, a notch may deepen until it becomes a sea cave. Waves may cut through the walls of sea caves to form sea arches. Arches may also form when waves cut through vertical cracks in narrow headlands. If the roof of a sea arch falls in, what remains is a tall, narrow rock island called a sea stack.

Sea caves, sea arches, and sea stacks can be seen on the coasts of California, Oregon, Washington, and Maine, on the Gaspé Peninsula of Canada, and in many parts of the Mediterranean Sea.

16.3

B **KEY IDEA**

Waves erode shorelines and deposit sediments in characteristic formations.

C **KEY VOCABULARY**

• beach
• sandbar
• fjord

BAJA PENINSULA Ocean waves have formed this sea stack and sea arch in Mexico.

D

Sea stack

Sea arch

349

Reading a Table

Tables give a lot of information in an organized way. These tips can help you read a table quickly and accurately. Look at the example as you read each strategy in this list.

A Look at the **title** to find out the content of the table.

B Read the **introduction** to get a general overview of the information included in the table.

C Examine the **heading** of each row and column. To find specific information, locate the place where a row and column intersect.

B Water temperatures vary widely along the coasts of North America. This table shows the temperature of the water in March at eight beaches.

A Average March Water Temperature at Eight Beaches (°F)

C Location	Temperature	Location	Temperature
Newport, RI	37	Oceanside, CA	58
Ocean City, MD	42	Seattle, WA	46
Veracruz, Mexico	75	Honolulu, HI	76
Freeport, TX	62	Juneau, AK	37

MARK IT UP Answer the following questions using the table of March water temperatures.

1. Which two beaches have the same water temperature? Circle the answers in the table.

2. What units are used to measure the water temperatures?

_____

_____

3. If you were planning a swimming vacation in March, what two beaches might you consider visiting?

_____

_____

Reading a Map

To read a map correctly, you have to identify and understand its elements. Look at the example below as you read each strategy in this list.

A Read the **title** to find out what the map shows.

B Study the **legend,** or **key,** to find out what symbols and colors are used on the map and what they stand for.

C Look at **geographic labels** to understand specific places on the map.

D Look at the **scale** to understand how distances on the map relate to actual distances.

E Locate the **compass rose,** or **pointer,** to determine direction.

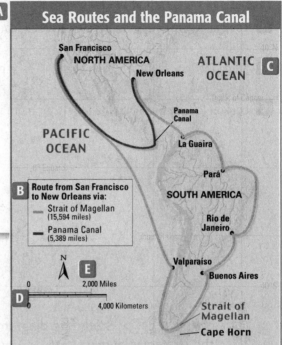

A Sea Routes and the Panama Canal

San Francisco
NORTH AMERICA
New Orleans
ATLANTIC OCEAN **C**
Panama Canal
PACIFIC OCEAN
La Guaira
Pará
SOUTH AMERICA
Rio de Janeiro
Valparaíso
Buenos Aires
Strait of Magellan
Cape Horn

B Route from San Francisco to New Orleans via:
— Strait of Magellan (15,594 miles)
— Panama Canal (5,389 miles)

N
E
0   2,000 Miles
D
0   4,000 Kilometers

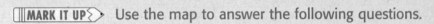

▓▓MARK IT UP▷ Use the map to answer the following questions.

1. What does this map show? _____

_____

_____

2. How many miles is the sea route from San Francisco to New Orleans by way of the Strait of Magellan?

_____

3. How many miles would you save by taking the Panama Canal from San Francisco to New Orleans rather than the route through the Strait of Magellan?

_____

4. Draw a straight line from San Francisco to New Orleans. About how many miles apart are these cities by land?

_____

Reading a Diagram

Diagrams combine pictures with a few words to provide a lot of information. Look at the example on the opposite page as you read each of the following strategies.

A Look at the **title** to get an idea of what the diagram is about.

B Study the **images** closely to understand each part of the diagram.

C Look at the **captions** and the **labels** for more information.

MARK IT UP Study the diagram, then answer the following questions using the strategies above.

1. What does this diagram illustrate? _____

_____

_____

2. What is one example of a composite volcano? _____

_____

_____

3. What is one difference between cinder cones and composite volcanoes?

_____

_____

4. Circle the name of the layer of the earth that lies under the continental crust.

5. Draw a box around the part of the diagram that shows the internal structure of a composite volcano.

A Volcanic Landforms

The shape and structure of a volcano are determined by the nature of its eruptions and the materials it ejects. A cinder cone, perhaps the simplest form of volcano, forms when molten lava is thrown into the air from a vent. Cinder cones, which tend to be smaller than other types of volcanoes, typically form in groups and on the sides of larger volcanoes. Composite volcanoes develop when layers of materials from successive eruptions accumulate around a vent. The diagram shows the structure of these two types of volcanoes.

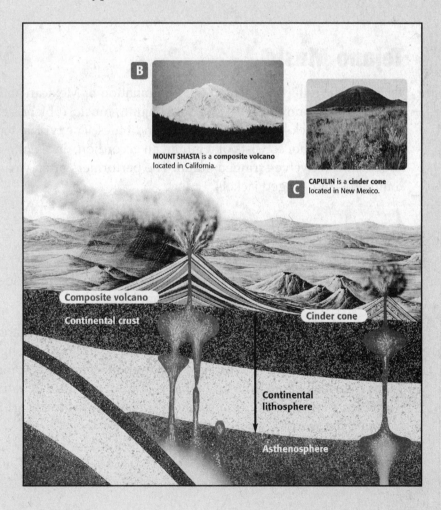

B

MOUNT SHASTA is a **composite volcano** located in California.

C CAPULIN is a **cinder cone** located in New Mexico.

Composite volcano

Continental crust

Cinder cone

Continental lithosphere

Asthenosphere

Main Idea and Supporting Details

The *main idea* in a paragraph is its most important point. *Details* in the paragraph support the main idea. Identifying the main idea will help you focus on the main message the writer wants to communicate. Use the following strategies to help you identify a paragraph's main idea and supporting details.

- Look for the **main idea,** which is often the first sentence in a paragraph.

- Use the main idea to help you **summarize** the point of the paragraph.

- Identify specific **details,** including facts and examples, that support the main idea.

Tejano Music

Main idea — Tejano music reflects a harmonious combination of Mexican and American lifestyles. Also known as Tex Mex or conjunto music, it blends elements of jazz, country, rock 'n' roll, and rhythm and blues. The typical tejano band, or conjunto tejano, consists of a guitar, an accordion, and a *bajo sexto*, or large Spanish twelve-stringed guitar. The performers often wear colorful sombreros and fringed jackets.

Details —

〰️**MARK IT UP** ⟩ Read the following paragraph. Circle the main idea. Then underline the details that support the main idea.

San Antonio, Texas, is a hub of tejano music. Many radio stations compete to bring listeners the latest recording artists and songs. On any given day, articles in numerous newspapers and magazines keep fans informed about who and what is hot. A San Antonio native, Flaco Jiménez, played an important role in spreading this lively art form around the world.

Problem and Solution

Does the proposed solution to a problem make sense? In order to decide, you need to look at each part of the text. Use the following strategies to read the text below.

- Look at the beginning or middle of a paragraph to find the **statement of the problem.**
- Find **details** that explain the problem and tell why it is important.
- Look for the **proposed solution.**
- Identify the **supporting details** for the proposed solution.
- Think about whether the solution is a good one.

Lunchroom Language Tables Can Beef Up Students' Skills
by Tara Blum

Statement of problem
Teachers, parents, administrators, and school board members are concerned that foreign language students are not getting enough practice actually using the language in conversation.

Details about the problem
In their foreign language classes, students read dialogs from their textbooks and respond to questions, but rarely get a chance to just communicate their thoughts.

Proposed solution
One way to address this problem would be to establish language tables in the lunchroom. Students taking a specific language would eat their lunch at a designated table one day a week. The only rule would be that they must speak no English, just the foreign language.

Details about the solution
This plan has several advantages. First, it doesn't require any additional equipment or materials. Second, it wouldn't take time away from other classes or activities. Language students have to eat lunch just like everyone else. Finally, it would be a lot of fun.

Language tables would let students supplement their language skills while nourishing their bodies. And that's a recipe for success!

MARK IT UP Use the text and strategies above to answer these questions.

1. Underline the proposed solution.

2. Circle at least one reason that supports this solution.

3. Explain why you think this is or is not a good solution to the problem.

_____

_____

_____

Sequence

Sequence is the order in which events happen. Whether you read a story or a social studies lesson, it is important for you to understand *when* things happen in relation to one another. The tips below can help you identify sequence in any type of text.

- Look for the **main steps** or **events** in the sequence.
- Look for **words and phrases that signal time**, such as *in 1845, two days later,* and *by fall of that year.*
- Look for **words and phrases that signal order**, such as *after, first,* and *meanwhile.*

MARK IT UP Read the passage about the war with Mexico on the next page. Then use the information from the article and the tips above to answer the questions.

1. Underline two words or phrases that signal time.

2. Circle two words or phrases that signal order.

3. A time line can help you identify and understand a sequence of events. Use the information from the passage to complete this time line.

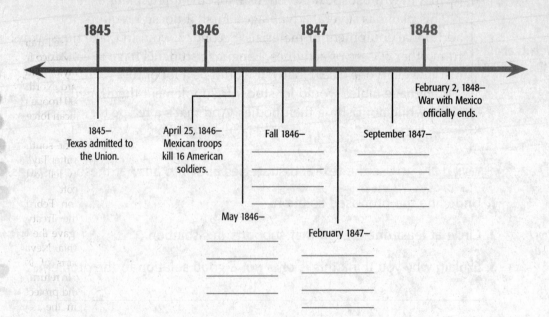

1845

1846

1847

1848

February 2, 1848—
War with Mexico
officially ends.

1845—
Texas admitted to
the Union.

April 25, 1846—
Mexican troops
kill 16 American
soldiers.

Fall 1846—
_____
_____
_____

September 1847—
_____
_____
_____

May 1846—
_____
_____
_____

February 1847—
_____
_____
_____

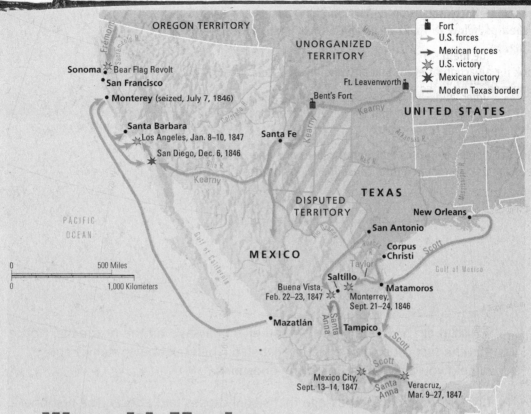

War with Mexico

In 1845, Congress admitted Texas to the Union as a slave state, despite Northern objections to the spread of slavery. However, Mexico still claimed Texas as its own. Mexico angrily viewed this annexation as an act of war.

In a diplomatic gesture, President Polk sent an ambassador to Mexico offering $25 million for Texas, California, and New Mexico. After Mexico refused, the U.S. sent troops to the northern bank of the Rio Grande. The Mexicans responded with troops on the southern bank. On April 25, 1846, a Mexican cavalry unit crossed the Rio Grande, ambushing an American patrol and killing 16 American soldiers. Two days later, Congress declared war.

U.S. troops entered Mexico in May 1846. About the same time, troops marched toward New Mexico. They took the territory without firing a shot. They then moved westward, and by fall of that year, Americans controlled all of New Mexico and California.

The defeat of Mexico proved far more difficult. The Mexican army was much larger, but the U.S. troops were led by well-trained officers. American forces invaded Mexico from two directions. First, General Taylor battled his way south from Texas toward Northern Mexico. In February 1847, his 4,800 troops met General Santa Anna's 15,000 Mexican forces at Buena Vista. Santa Anna retreated.

Meanwhile, a fierce battle for southern Mexico was raging. Seven months after Taylor's victory in the North, Mexico City fell to U.S. troops led by General Winfield Scott.

The war officially ended on February 2, 1848, with the signing of the Treaty of Guadalupe Hidalgo. This treaty gave the U.S. the present-day states of California, Nevada, Utah, most of Arizona, and parts of New Mexico, Colorado, and Wyoming. In return, the U.S. offered Mexico $15 million and protection of the 80,000 Mexicans living in the newly acquired territories.

Cause and Effect

A *cause* is an event that brings about another event. An *effect* is something that happens as a result of the first event. Identifying causes and effects helps you understand how events are related. Use the tips below to find causes and effects in any kind of reading.

- Look for an action or event that answers the question, "What happened?" This is the **effect.**

- Look for an action or event that answers the question, "Why did this happen?" This is the **cause.**

- Look for words or phrases that **signal** causes and effects, such as *because, as a result, therefore, consequently,* and *since.*

MARK IT UP Read the cause-and-effect passage on the next page. Notice that the first cause and effect are labeled. Then use the strategies above to help you answer the following questions.

1. Circle words in the passage that signal causes and effects. The first one has been done for you.

2. Some causes may have more than one effect. What are two effects of the mosquito's saliva on the body of the victim?

_____

_____

3. Complete the following diagram showing the cause and effects of mosquito bites.

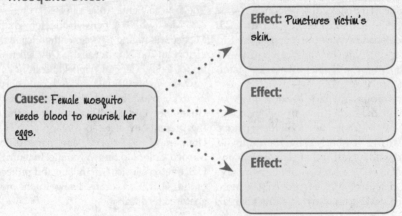

Effect: Punctures victim's skin

Cause: Female mosquito needs blood to nourish her eggs.

Effect:

Effect:

Bzz! Slap!

Cause
If you spend any time outdoors in the summer, at some point you will probably find yourself covered with mosquito bites. The word *mosquito* means "little fly" in Spanish, but the impact these pesky insects have on people is anything but small.

Signal Word
Effect
Mosquitoes can transmit serious diseases such as yellow fever, encephalitis, and malaria. Usually, though, mosquito bites just (cause) people to develop raised, red bumps that itch like crazy.

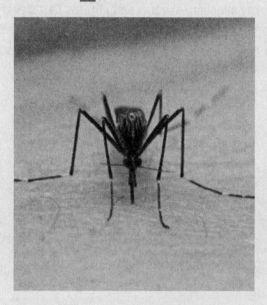

This is what happens. Female mosquitoes need blood to nourish the eggs developing in their bodies. Consequently, they zero in on living things whose blood they can suck. Once they find a likely victim, the attack begins.

This attack is not really a bite, since a mosquito isn't able to open her jaws. Instead, she punctures the victim's skin with sharp stylets inside her mouth. The mosquito's saliva then flows into these puncture wounds. Because the saliva keeps the victim's blood from clotting, the mosquito can drink her fill. This can sometimes amount to 150 percent of the mosquito's weight.

Meanwhile, the mosquito's saliva sets off an allergic reaction in the victim. As a result, the person develops the itchy swelling we call a mosquito bite. Ironically, if the mosquito finishes eating before the victim slaps or drives her off, there will be less saliva left in the skin. Therefore, the allergic reaction and itching will not be so severe.

Here are some steps you can take to help prevent mosquito bites or lessen their effect if you do get bitten.

- Don't go out at prime mosquito time—from dusk to dawn.
- Use insect repellent at all times.
- If you do get bitten, DON'T SCRATCH. Scratching just increases the allergic reaction.

Comparison and Contrast

Comparing two things means showing how they are the same.
Contrasting two things means showing how they are different.
Comparisons and contrasts are important because they show
how things or ideas are related. Use these tips to help you
understand comparison and contrast in reading assignments such
as the article on the opposite page.

- Look for **direct statements** of **comparison and contrast.** "These
  things are similar because…" or "One major difference is…"

- Pay attention to **words and phrases that signal comparisons,**
  such as *also, both, is the same as,* and *in the same way.*

- Notice **words and phrases that signal contrasts.** Some of these
  are *however, still, but,* and *in contrast.*

MARK IT UP Read the article on the next page. Then use the information
from the article and the tips above to answer the questions.

1. Circle the words and phrases that signal comparisons. A sample has been
   done for you.

2. Underline the words and phrases that signal contrast. Notice the sample
   that has been done.

3. A Venn diagram shows how two subjects are similar and how they are
   different. Complete this diagram, which uses information from the article
   to compare and contrast *la quinceañera* and a sweet sixteen party. Add
   one or more similarities to the center of the diagram and one or more
   differences to each outer circle.

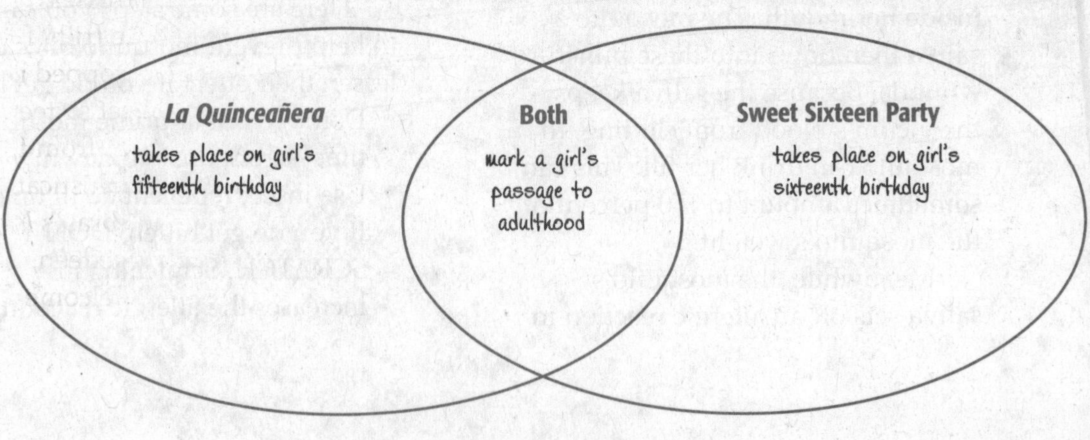

La Quinceañera

takes place on girl's
fifteenth birthday

Both

mark a girl's
passage to
adulthood

Sweet Sixteen Party

takes place on girl's
sixteenth birthday

La Quinceañera and Sweet Sixteen

Almost every culture has a ceremony to mark the passage of young people from childhood to adulthood. In the Latin culture, this rite of passage for girls is *la quinceañera*. For American girls, it is the sweet sixteen birthday party.

Comparison Although both *la quinceañera* and the sweet sixteen birthday party commemorate a girl's passage to **Contrast** adulthood, they <u>differ</u> in when, where, and how the occasion is celebrated. *Quinceañera* means "fifteenth birthday," and that's when the celebration is held. In contrast, a sweet sixteen party takes place when, as the name suggests, a girl is a year older.

The origin of *la quinceañera* is uncertain, although it may have roots in the Aztec, Maya, or Toltec cultures. It generally involves celebration of a thanksgiving Mass followed by a lavish party for the extended family and friends. The *quinceañera* often dances a waltz with her father and other male relatives. In Mexico, girlfriends may give the celebrant a rag doll symbolizing her leaving childhood and its toys behind.

Sweet sixteen parties, on the other hand, do not include the religious component of *la quinceañera*. They also tend to be designed for the girl's friends rather than for her family. Like *quinceañeras*, however, they often are held in hotels or reception halls and include live bands, plentiful food, and many-tiered birthday cakes.

Both *quinceañeras* and sweet sixteeners take advantage of the opportunity to look as adult as possible. They generally deck themselves out in long dresses. *Quinceañeras* often choose frilly frocks in white or pastel colors topped by hats or headdresses. Sweet sixteen dresses can run the gamut from frothy and frilly to sleek and sophisticated.

So whether a girl celebrates *la quinceañera* or her sweet sixteen, the message is the same—"Welcome to adulthood!"

Persuasion

To be persuasive, an opinion should be backed up with reasons and facts. After you carefully read an opinion and the reasons and facts that support it, you will be able to decide if the opinion makes sense. As you read these tips, look at the sample persuasive essay on the next page.

- Look for words or phrases that **signal an opinion**, such as *I believe, I think,* and *in my opinion.*

- Identify reasons, facts, or expert opinions that **support** the position.

- Ask yourself if the opinion and the reasons that back it up **make sense.**

- Look for **errors in reasoning,** such as overgeneralizations, that may affect the presentation of the opinion.

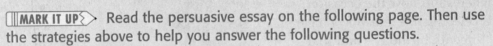 Read the persuasive essay on the following page. Then use the strategies above to help you answer the following questions.

1. Underline any words or phrases that signal the writer's opinion.

2. Circle any words or phrases that signal the opinion of persons other than the writer.

3. The writer presents both sides of this debate. List the points supporting both sides in the chart below. One reason has been provided for you.

For swimming pool	Against swimming pool
1. The school has a responsibility to teach swimming.	

Our School Needs to Get in the Swim *by Jorge Rojo*

This school needs a swimming pool. Swimming is an important life skill and I believe it is the responsibility of the school to provide this essential part of students' education.

The school's mission is to educate the whole person—mind and body—and to prepare students to be productive citizens. In addition to our academic subjects, we are taught how to eat right, budget our money, and drive a car. But we don't learn the water safety skills that could someday save our lives.

The community and school board obviously don't feel the way I do, however. They repeatedly have refused to fund the building of a pool. In the opinion of one board member, "Students can take swimming lessons at the local health club." Other school officials think that the school has more important needs—repairing the sagging gym floor and installing new lockers, for example.

In my opinion, these reasons are not valid. First, most students cannot afford lessons at the health club. Even those who have the money don't have the time. They're busy with homework and other activities during the school year and have to work or go to summer school during vacation.

I agree that the gym floor should be replaced and wouldn't mind having a new locker. But I believe that the educational needs of the students should come first. Swimming is one of the best forms of exercise there is. Even if knowing how to swim never saves your life, it can improve its quality. Isn't that what an education is all about?

Social studies class becomes easier when you understand how your textbook's words, pictures, and maps work together to give you information. Following these tips can make you a better reader of social studies lessons. As you read the tips, look at the sample lesson on the right-hand page.

A Read the **title** of the lesson and other **headings** to find out what the lesson is about. Smaller headings may introduce subtopics that are related to the main topic.

B Read the **main ideas** or **objectives** listed on the first page of the lesson. These items summarize the lesson and help set a purpose for your reading.

C Look at the **vocabulary terms** listed on the lesson's first page. These terms will be boldfaced or underlined where they appear in the text.

D Notice **how information is organized.** In social studies lessons, ideas are often presented using sequence, cause and effect, comparison and contrast, and main idea and supporting details.

E Carefully examine **visuals** such as photographs, boxed text, maps, charts, bulleted lists, time lines, and diagrams. Think about how the visuals and the text are related.

|||MARK IT UP⟩ Carefully read the textbook page on the right. Use the information from the text and from the tips above to answer the questions.

1. What is the topic of this lesson? _____

_____

2. Circle the main idea of the lesson.

3. List two details about César Chávez's life. _____

_____

_____

4. Underline the sentence that tells what farm workers did to protest poor pay.

5. What information does the quotation in the tinted box add to the text?

_____

_____

③ The Equal Rights Struggle Expands

C TERMS & NAMES
César Chávez
National Congress of American Indians
Betty Friedan
NOW
ERA

B MAIN IDEA

The African-American struggle for equality inspired other groups to fight for equality.

WHY IT MATTERS NOW

Nonwhites and women continue to fight for equality today.

ONE AMERICAN'S STORY

César Chávez was born in Yuma, Arizona, in 1927. In the 1940s, he and his family worked as migrant laborers in the California fields. (Migrant workers travel from place to place in search of work.) One time, they found work picking peas. The whole family, parents and six children, worked. Chávez described the poor pay for such hard work.

César Chávez, head of the National Farm Workers Association, marches with striking grape pickers in the 1960s. (*Huelga* is the Spanish word for strike.)

A VOICE FROM THE PAST

They [the managers] would take only the peas they thought were good, and they only paid you for those. The pay was twenty cents a hamper, which had to weigh in at twenty-five pounds. So in about three hours, the whole family made only twenty cents.

César Chávez, *César Chávez: Autobiography of* La Causa

In 1962, Chávez decided to start a union for farm workers. But the owners refused to recognize the union. Chávez used the example set by Martin Luther King, Jr., to change their minds.

D Responding to Chávez's call, workers went on strike. Then Chávez asked people not to buy produce harvested by nonunion workers. The tactics worked. In 1970, 26 major California growers signed a contract with the union. It gave the workers higher wages and new benefits. The victory of Chávez and his union showed how the fight for equal rights spread beyond African Americans, as you will read in this section.

A Mexican Americans Organize

The farm workers' struggle inspired other Mexican Americans. By the 1960s, most Mexican Americans lived in cities in the Southwest and California. In 1970, Mexican Americans formed *La Raza Unida* (lah RAH•sah oo•NEE•dah)—"the united people." *La Raza* fought for better jobs, pay, education, and housing. It also worked to elect Mexican Americans to public office.

Mexican-American students also began to organize. They wanted reform in the school system. The students demanded such changes as

Reading a science textbook becomes easier when you understand how the explanations, drawings, and special terms work together. Use the strategies below to help you better understand your science textbook. Look at the examples on the opposite page as you read each strategy in this list.

A Preview the **title** and any **headings** to see what scientific concepts you will learn about.

B Read the **key ideas** or **objectives.** These items summarize the lesson and help set a purpose for your reading.

C Read the list of **vocabulary terms** that will be introduced and defined in the lesson.

D Notice the **boldfaced** and **italicized** terms in the text. Look for the definitions of these terms.

E Carefully examine any **pictures** or **diagrams.** Read the **captions** to see how the graphics help to illustrate the text.

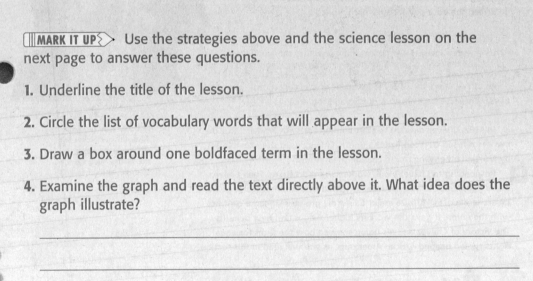

MARK IT UP Use the strategies above and the science lesson on the next page to answer these questions.

1. Underline the title of the lesson.

2. Circle the list of vocabulary words that will appear in the lesson.

3. Draw a box around one boldfaced term in the lesson.

4. Examine the graph and read the text directly above it. What idea does the graph illustrate?

_____

_____

5. At what latitude is the elevation of the snow line lowest?

_____

_____

15.1

B KEY IDEAS

Glaciers are huge ice masses that move under the influence of gravity.

Glaciers form from compacted and recrystallized snow.

C KEY VOCABULARY
- glacier
- snow line
- firn
- valley glacier
- continental glacier
- ice cap

![i] VISUALIZATIONS
CLASSZONE.COM

Examine seasonal migration of snow cover.
Keycode: ES1501

E

VOCABULARY STRATEGY

The word *firn* comes from a German word meaning "last year's snow." The word *névé* is related to a Latin word meaning "cooled by snow."

A ## What Is a Glacier?

About 75 percent of Earth's fresh water is frozen in glaciers. A **glacier** is a large mass of compacted snow and ice that moves under the force of gravity. A glacier changes Earth's surface as it erodes geological features in one place and then redeposits the material elsewhere thus altering the landscape.

Where Glaciers Form

Glaciers form in areas that are always covered by snow. In such areas, more snow falls than melts each year; as a result layers of snow build up from previous years. Climates cold enough to cause such conditions may be found in any part of the world. Air temperatures drop as you climb high above sea level and as you travel farther from the equator.

Even in equatorial areas, however, a layer of permanent snow may exist on high mountains at high elevation. Farther from the equator, the elevation need not be so high for a layer of permanent snow to exist. In the polar areas, permanent snow may be found even at sea level. The lowest elevation at which the layer of permanent snow occurs in summer is called **D** the **snow line.** If a mountain is completely covered with snow in winter but without snow in summer, it has no snow line.

In general, the snow line occurs at lower and lower elevations as the latitudes approach the poles. The snow line also changes according to total yearly snowfall and the amount of solar exposure. Thus, the elevation of the snow line is not the same for all places at a given latitude.

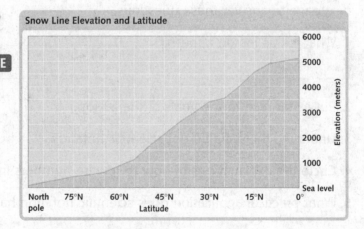

Snow Line Elevation and Latitude

(graph: Latitude from North pole, 75°N, 60°N, 45°N, 30°N, 15°N, 0°; Elevation (meters) from Sea level, 1000, 2000, 3000, 4000, 5000, 6000)

How Glaciers Form

Except for bare rock cliffs, a mountain above the snow line is always buried in snow. Great basins below the highest peaks are filled with snow that can be hundreds of meters thick. In these huge snowfields, buried snow becomes compressed and recrystallizes into a rough, granular ice material called **firn** (feern) or névé (nay-VAY).

Reading in mathematics is different from reading in history, literature, or science. A math lesson has few words, but instead illustrates math concepts using numbers, symbols, formulas, equations, diagrams, and word problems. Use the following strategies, and the lesson on the next page, to help you better understand your math textbook.

A Scan the **title** and **headings** to see which math concepts you will learn about.

B Look for **goals, objectives** or **key ideas**. These help focus your reading.

C Read **explanations** carefully. Sometimes a concept is explained in more than one way to make sure you understand it.

D Look for **special features** such as study or technology tips or connections to real life. These provide more help or information.

E Study any **worked-out solutions** to sample problems. These are the key to understanding how to do the homework assignment.

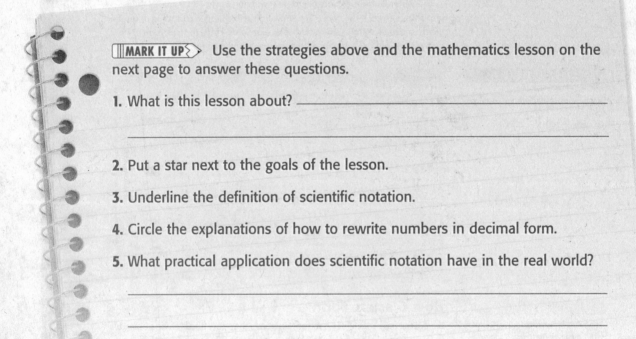

▌▌▌**MARK IT UP** ⟩ Use the strategies above and the mathematics lesson on the next page to answer these questions.

1. What is this lesson about? _____

_____

2. Put a star next to the goals of the lesson.

3. Underline the definition of scientific notation.

4. Circle the explanations of how to rewrite numbers in decimal form.

5. What practical application does scientific notation have in the real world?

_____

_____

8.4

B *What you should learn*

GOAL 1 Use scientific notation to represent numbers.

GOAL 2 Use scientific notation to describe **real-life** situations, such as the price per acre of the Alaska purchase in **Example 6**.

D *Why you should learn it*

▼ To solve **real-life** problems, such as finding the amount of water discharged by the Amazon River each year in **Example 5**.

Scientific Notation

GOAL 1 USING SCIENTIFIC NOTATION

A number is written in **scientific notation** if it is of the form $c \times 10^n$, where $1 \le c < 10$ and n is an integer. **C**

▶ **ACTIVITY**

Developing Concepts

Investigating Scientific Notation

1. Rewrite each number in decimal form.

   a. 6.43×10^4 **b.** 3.072×10^6 **c.** 4.2×10^{-2} **d.** 1.52×10^{-3}

2. Describe a general rule for writing the decimal form of a number given in scientific notation. How many places do you move the decimal point? Do you move the decimal point left or right?

EXAMPLE 1 *Rewriting in Decimal Form*

Rewrite in decimal form.

a. 2.834×10^2 **b.** 4.9×10^5 **c.** 7.8×10^{-1} **d.** 1.23×10^{-6}

SOLUTION **E**

a. $2.834 \times 10^2 = 283.4$ Move decimal point right 2 places.

b. $4.9 \times 10^5 = 490,000$ Move decimal point right 5 places.

c. $7.8 \times 10^{-1} = 0.78$ Move decimal point left 1 place.

d. $1.23 \times 10^{-6} = 0.00000123$ Move decimal point left 6 places.

EXAMPLE 2 *Rewriting in Scientific Notation*

a. $34,690 = 3.469 \times 10^4$ Move decimal point left 4 places.

b. $1.78 = 1.78 \times 10^0$ Move decimal point 0 places.

c. $0.039 = 3.9 \times 10^{-2}$ Move decimal point right 2 places.

d. $0.000722 = 7.22 \times 10^{-4}$ Move decimal point right 4 places.

e. $5,600,000,000 = 5.6 \times 10^9$ Move decimal point left 9 places.

Reading an Application

To get a part-time job or to register for summer camp or classes at the local community center, you will have to fill out an application. Being able to understand the format of an application will help you fill it out correctly. Use the following strategies and the sample on the next page to help you understand any application.

A **Begin at the top.** Scan the application to understand the different sections.

B Look for special **instructions for filling out** the application.

C Note any **request for materials** or **special information** that must be included with the application.

D Watch for **sections you don't have to fill in** or **questions you don't have to answer.**

E Look for difficult or confusing words or abbreviations. Look them up in a dictionary or ask someone what they mean.

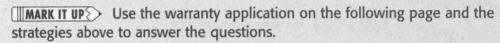 **MARK IT UP** Use the warranty application on the following page and the strategies above to answer the questions.

1. Why is it important to fill out and mail this warranty application?

_____

_____

2. Underline the phrase that tells when the application must be mailed.

3. What information about the product do you have to supply?

_____

4. Circle the part of the application that you do not have to fill out.

5. What purchase document must you use to fill out this application?

_____

6. ASSESSMENT PRACTICE Circle the letter of the correct answer.
What amount should you include in the box marked "retail price paid"?

A. the total amount you paid for the product

B. the total amount you paid minus the cost of the maintenance agreement

C. the price marked on the product

D. the cost of extra charges, such as delivery and installation

A Congratulations on investing in a Calvo product. Your decision will reward you for years to come. Please complete your Warranty Registration Card to ensure that you receive all the privileges and protection that come with your purchase.

Your completed Warranty Registration Card serves as confirmation of ownership in the event of theft.

Returning the attached card guarantees you'll receive all the special offers for which your purchase makes you eligible.

- **DETACH AND MAIL PORTION BELOW.** -

USA Limited Warranty Registration	
123456 XXXX	ABCDEFG7654321
MODEL NUMBER	SERIAL NUMBER

Registering your product ensures that you receive all of the benefits you are entitled to as a Calvo customer. Complete the information below in ink, and drop this card in the nearest mailbox.

B ■ IMPORTANT - RETURN WITHIN TEN DAYS

Date of Purchase

Your Name
First | Initial | Last

Address
Street | Apt. #

City | State | ZIP Code

C **Retail Price Paid** $ _____ .00
(Excluding sales tax, maintenance agreement, delivery, installation, and trade-in allowance.) **E**

D **Your Phone Number** (optional)
Area Code | Phone Number

CALVO

Reading a Public Notice

Public notices can tell you about events in your community and give you valuable information about safety. When you read a public notice, follow these tips. Each tip relates to a specific part of the notice on the next page.

A Read the notice's **title,** if it has one. The title often gives the main idea or purpose of the notice.

B See if there is a logo, credit, or other way of telling **who created the notice.**

C Ask yourself, **"Who should read this notice?"** If the information in it might be important to you or someone you know, then you should pay attention to it.

D Look for **contact information** that indicates where to get answers to questions.

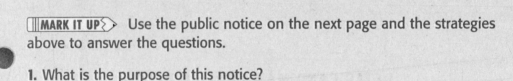 **MARK IT UP** Use the public notice on the next page and the strategies above to answer the questions.

1. What is the purpose of this notice?

_____

2. Circle the name of the organization that created the notice.

3. Who does this notice apply to?

_____

4. Make a star next to the contact information.

5. Who should get a flu shot earliest—health care workers or healthy people 50–64 years old?

_____

6. ASSESSMENT PRACTICE Circle the letter of the correct answer.
The best time to get a flu shot is
   A. your doctor's decision
   B. October or November
   C. October
   D. December

A When should *YOU* get your flu shot?

C	OCT	NOV	DEC or later
People at high risk of severe illness ✓ **65 years old or older**—Even in you're in great health ✓ **Children 6–23 months old**—Children younger than 2 years old have one of the highest rates of hospitalizations from influenza ✓ **Adults and children with a chronic health condition**—Such as heart disease, diabetes, kidney disease, asthma, cancer, and HIV/AIDS ✓ **More than 3 months pregnant during flu season**—Typically November through March	**Best Time**		**Not too late!**
People who can give the flu to those at high risk ✓ **Household contact or caregiver of someone at high risk** ✓ **Health care workers** ✓ **Household contact or caregiver of a child under 2 years old**—Infants younger than 6 months old can't get a flu shot, but they can get the flu	**Best Time**		**Not too late!**
Your child's very first flu shot ✓ **Children 6 months–8 years old** getting the very first flu shot need a booster shot one month after the first dose of vaccine	**Best Time**		**Not too late!**
Healthy people 50–64 years old		**Best Time**	**Not too late!**
Anyone who wants to prevent the flu		**Best Time**	**Not too late!**

A flu shot is your best protection against the flu.

For more information: Ask your health care provider or call the CDC Immunization Hotline.
English: 1-800-232-2522   Español: 1-800-232-0233   www.cdc.gov/nip/flu D

 B **CDC Immunization** SAFER • HEALTHIER • PEOPLE

Fight the Flu

Reading a Web Page

When you research information for a report or project, you may use the World Wide Web. Once you find the site you want, the strategies below will help you find the facts and details you need. Look at the sample Web page on the right as you read each of the strategies.

A Notice the page's **Web address,** or URL. Write down the Web address or bookmark it if you think you might return to the page at another time or if you need to add it to a list of sources.

B Read the **title** of the page. The title usually tells you what topics the page covers.

C Look for **menu bars** along the top, bottom, or side of the page. These guide you to other parts of the site that may be useful.

D Notice any **links** to other parts of the site or to related pages. Links are often highlighted in color or underlined.

E Many sites have a link that allows you to **contact** the creators with questions or feedback.

F Use a **search feature** to find out quickly whether the information you want to locate appears anywhere on the site.

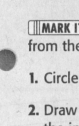 **MARK IT UP** Look at the Web page on the right. Then use the information from the Web page and the tips above to answer the questions.

1. Circle the Web address of this site.

2. Draw boxes around two places you can search the site to see if it contains the information you need.

3. What is the name of the president of NLN? _____

4. Put a star by the link you should click on to make an online contribution to NLN.

5. ASSESSMENT PRACTICE Circle the letter of the best answer.
This site is designed to give information about
A. issues of interest to Latinos
B. Latino education
C. raising Latino children
D. politicians Latinos should vote for

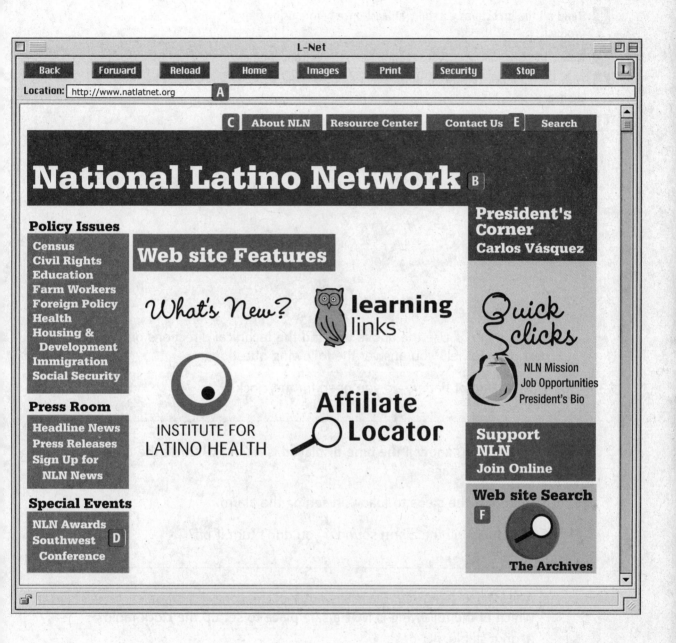

L-Net

Back | Forward | Reload | Home | Images | Print | Security | Stop | L

Location: http://www.natlatnet.org A

C About NLN | Resource Center | Contact Us E | Search

National Latino Network B

President's Corner
Carlos Vásquez

Policy Issues

Census
Civil Rights
Education
Farm Workers
Foreign Policy
Health
Housing & Development
Immigration
Social Security

Web site Features

What's New?

learning links

Quick clicks

NLN Mission
Job Opportunities
President's Bio

INSTITUTE FOR LATINO HEALTH

Affiliate Locator

Press Room

Headline News
Press Releases
Sign Up for NLN News

Support NLN
Join Online

Special Events

NLN Awards
Southwest D
Conference

Web site Search F

The Archives

Reading Technical Directions

Reading technical directions will help you understand how to use the products you buy. Use the following tips to help you read a variety of technical directions.

A Look carefully at any **diagrams** or **other images** of the product.

B **Read all the directions** carefully at least once before using the product.

C Notice **headings** or **lines** that separate one section from another.

D Look for **numbers, letters,** or **bullets** that give the steps in sequence.

E Watch for **warnings** or **notes** with more information.

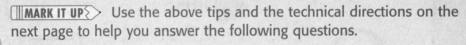 Use the above tips and the technical directions on the next page to help you answer the following questions.

1. What kind of battery do you need for the clock?

_____

2. How do you know if the time displayed is AM or PM? Circle the answer on the next page.

3. Underline the steps to follow in setting the alarm.

4. How long will the alarm sound if you don't turn it off?

_____

5. **ASSESSMENT PRACTICE** Circle the letter of the correct answer.
   Which of the following is NOT a safe place to set up the clock radio?
   A. on a stable, flat desk
   B. in the bathroom
   C. away from open windows
   D. on a bedside table

Alarm Clock Radio
INSTRUCTIONS FOR USE

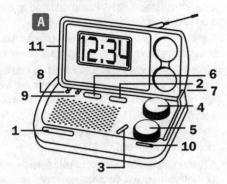

1. SNOOZE/LIGHT BUTTON
2. FUNCTION SWITCH
3. BAND SWITCH
4. TUNING CONTROL
5. VOLUME CONTROL
6. TIME/ALARM SET SWITCH
7. BATTERY DOOR (RADIO)
8. HOUR BUTTON
9. MINUTE BUTTON
10. EJECT BUTTON
11. BATTERY HOLDER (CLOCK)

BATTERIES
FOR RADIO:

To insert batteries, remove the BATTERY DOOR (7) and insert 2 AAA batteries, observing the correct position of the polarity.

FOR CLOCK:

Pull out the BATTERY HOLDER (11). Use a 1.5 volt battery and place with positive electrode facing front. Reinsert battery holder.

C HOW TO PLAY THE RADIO

- Press the EJECT BUTTON (10) to open lid.
- Turn the FUNCTION SWITCH (2) TO "ON" position.
- Use the BAND SWITCH (3) to select broadcasting band (AM or FM).
- Turn the TUNING CONTROL knob (4) to select the listening station.

D TO SET THE TIME

- Slide the TIME/ALARM SET SWITCH (6) to the "T.SET" position.
- Depress the HOUR BUTTON (8) until the correct hour is displayed. Be careful to set time to AM or PM as required. When PM time is registered, a "P" will appear on the display
- Depress the MINUTE BUTTON (9) until the correct minute is reached.

TO SET THE ALARM

- Slide the TIME/ALARM SET SWITCH (6) to the "AL.SET" position. "AL" indicator will appear on the display.
- Depress the HOUR BUTTON (8) until the desired alarm hour is displayed. Be careful to correctly set alarm to AM or PM as required. When PM time is registered, a "P" will appear on the display.
- Depress the MINUTE BUTTON (9) until the desired alarm time is reached.

WAKE TO ALARM

- Set the FUNCTION SWITCH (2) TO "ALARM" position. When the desired alarm time is reached, you will hear a sequential "BEEP" alarm for 60 seconds.
- To shut the alarm off temporarily, press the SNOOZE/LIGHT BUTTON (1) once. The alarm will stop for 4 minutes, then come on again.
- To stop the alarm completely, set the FUNCTION SWITCH (2) to "OFF" position.

WAKE TO MUSIC

- Set the FUNCTION SWITCH (2) TO "AUTO" position.
- The radio will turn on automatically at your desired alarm time.

SAFETY PRECAUTIONS E

- Do not place the unit near a moisture environment, such as a bathtub, kitchen, sink, etc. The unit should be well protected from rain, dew, condensation, or any form of dampness.
- Do not place the unit on surfaces with strong vibration. Place the unit only on flat, stable, and level surfaces.

Product Information: Directions for Use

Many of the products you buy come with instructions that tell you how to use them correctly. Directions for use may appear on the product itself, on its packaging, or on a separate insert. Learning to read and follow directions for use is important for your safety. As you read each strategy below, look at the sample.

A Read any **headings** to find out what kinds of information are given with the product.

B Read the directions, which usually tell you *why, how, when,* and *where* to use the product, *how much to use, how often,* and *when* to stop using it.

C Carefully read any **warnings** given with the product. The manufacturer will usually tell you what to do if you experience any problems.

D Look for any **contact information** that tells you where to call or write if you have a question about the product.

Solution of Hydrogen Peroxide 3% U.S.P.

Active ingredient: Hydrogen peroxide 3% **A**

Inactive ingredients: 0.001% Phosphoric Acid as a stabilizer and purified water

Indications: For topical use to help prevent infection in minor cuts, burns, and abrasions, or to cleanse the mouth.

Directions: Apply locally to affected areas. To cleanse the mouth, dilute with an equal amount of water and use as a **B** gargle or rinse. Do not use in excess of ten consecutive days.

Warnings: **C**

- FOR EXTERNAL USE: Topically to the skin and mucous membranes. KEEP OUT OF EYES.
- If redness, irritation, swelling, or pain persists or increases or if infection occurs, discontinue use and consult a physician.
- KEEP THIS AND ALL DRUGS OUT OF THE REACH OF CHILDREN. **In case of accidental ingestion, seek professional assistance or contact a Poison Control Center immediately**.

Storage: Keep bottle tightly closed and at controlled room temperature 59°–86° F (15°–30° C). Do not shake bottle.

Questions? (888) 555-1234 **D**

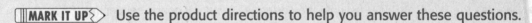

MARK IT UP Use the product directions to help you answer these questions.

1. How do you use the product to cleanse your mouth? _____

_____

2. Circle the active ingredient in this product.

3. What should you do if someone accidentally swallows this product? Underline the answer.

4. Draw a box around the number you should call if you have questions about the product.

5. ASSESSMENT PRACTICE Circle the letter of the correct answer. When should you stop using this product?

A. when the temperature drops below 59° F

B. if pain and swelling increase

C. if you have a minor abrasion

D. ten days after you buy it

Reading a Bus Schedule

Knowing how to read a bus schedule accurately can help you get where you need to go—on time. Look at the sample bus schedule as you read the tips below.

A Look at the **title** to know what the schedule covers.

B Identify **labels** that show **dates** or **days of the week** to help you understand how the daily or weekly schedule works.

C Look at **place labels** to know what stops are listed on the schedule.

D Look for **expressions of time** to know what hours or minutes are listed on the schedule.

E Pay attention to the **organization** of the information. Read across the row to see when a bus will reach each location.

A Route 238 Quincy Center Station - Holbrook/Randolph Commuter Rail Station via Crawford Sq.

WEEKDAY MORNINGS **B**

C Leave Quincy Station	Leave S. Shore Plaza	Leave Crawford Square	Arrive Holb./Rand. Commuter Rail Sta.	Leave Holb./Rand. Commuter Rail Sta.	Leave Crawford Square	Leave S. Shore Plaza	Arrive Quincy Station
D 5:25A	5:43A	5:58A	...	6:25A	6:29A	6:42A	7:08A
6:10	6:28	6:43	6:47A	6:50	6:54	7:07	7:35
6:25	6:43	6:58	7:03	7:20	7:25	7:38	8:06
6:45	7:03	7:19	7:24	7:50	7:55	8:08	8:36
7:05	7:25	7:41	7:46	8:25	8:30	8:43	9:11 **E**
7:30	7:50	8:06	8:11	8:55	9:00	9:13	9:41
7:55	8:15	8:31	8:36	9:25	9:30	9:46	10:14
8:15	8:35	8:51	8:56	10:05	10:10	10:26	10:54
9:10	9:30	9:46	9:51	11:00	11:05	11:21	11:49
10:05	10:25	10:41	10:46				
10:55	11:15	11:31	11:36				

MARK IT UP Use the bus schedule and the strategies on this page to answer the following questions.

1. Circle the name of one stop on this route.

   _____

   _____

2. What time does the last bus leave Quincy Station for Holb./Rand. Commuter Rail Station on weekday mornings?

   _____

3. If you took the 7:25 AM bus from Crawford Square, when would you arrive at Quincy Station?

4. **ASSESSMENT PRACTICE** Circle the letter of the correct answer. If you have a 10:15 meeting at S. Shore Plaza on Tuesday, what's the latest bus you can take from Holb./Rand. Commuter Rail Station?

   A. 8:25   **B.** 8:55   **C.** 9:25   **D.** 10:05

Test Preparation Strategies

In this section you'll find strategies and practice to help you with many different kinds of standardized tests. The strategies apply to questions based on long and short readings, as well as questions about charts, graphs, and product labels. You'll also find examples and practice for revising-and-editing tests and writing tests. Applying the strategies to the practice materials and thinking through the answers will help you succeed in many formal testing situations.

Test Preparation Strategies

You can prepare for tests in several ways. First, study and understand the content that will be on the test. Second, learn as many test-taking techniques as you can. These techniques will help you better understand the questions and how to answer them. Following are some general suggestions for preparing for and taking tests. Starting on page 160, you'll find more detailed suggestions and test-taking practice.

Successful Test Taking

 Study Content Throughout the Year

1. **Master the content of your class.** The best way to study for tests is to read, understand, and review the content of your class. Read your daily assignments carefully. Study the notes that you have taken in class. Participate in class discussions. Work with classmates in small groups to help one another learn. You might trade writing assignments and comment on your classmates' work.

2. **Use your textbook for practice.** Your textbook includes many different types of questions. Some may ask you to talk about a story you just read. Others may ask you to figure out what's wrong with a sentence or how to make a paragraph sound better. Try answering these questions out loud and in writing. This type of practice can make taking a test much easier.

3. **Learn how to understand the information in charts, maps, and graphic organizers.** One type of test question may ask you to look at a graphic organizer, such as a spider map, and explain something about the information you see there. Another type of question may ask you to look at a map to find a particular place. You'll find charts, maps, and graphic organizers to study in your textbook. You'll also find charts, maps, and graphs in your science, mathematics, literature, and social studies textbooks. When you look at these, ask yourself, What information is being presented and why is it important?

4. **Practice taking tests.** Use copies of tests you have taken in the past or in other classes for practice. Every test has a time limit, so set a timer for 15 or 20 minutes and then begin your practice. Try to finish the test in the time you've given yourself.

☑ **Reading Check** In what practical way can your textbook help you prepare for a test?

5. **Talk about test-taking experiences.** After you've taken a classroom test or quiz, talk about it with your teacher and classmates. Which types of questions were the hardest to understand? What made them difficult? Which questions seemed easiest, and why? When you share test-taking techniques with your classmates, everyone can become a successful test taker.

Use Strategies During the Test

1. **Read the directions carefully.** You can't be a successful test taker unless you know exactly what you are expected to do. Look for key words and phrases, such as *circle the best answer, write a paragraph,* or *choose the word that best completes each sentence.*

2. **Learn how to read test questions.** Test questions can sometimes be difficult to figure out. They may include unfamiliar language or be written in an unfamiliar way. Try rephrasing the question in a simpler way using words you understand. Always ask yourself, What type of information does this question want me to provide?

3. **Pay special attention when using a separate answer sheet.** If you accidentally skip a line on an answer sheet, all the rest of your answers may be wrong! Try one or more of the following techniques:

   - Use a ruler on the answer sheet to make sure you are placing your answers on the correct line.

   - After every five answers, check to make sure you're on the right line.

   - Each time you turn a page of the test booklet, check to make sure the number of the question is the same as the number of the answer line on the answer sheet.

   - If the answer sheet has circles, fill them in neatly. A stray pencil mark might cause the scoring machine to count the answer as incorrect.

4. **If you're not sure of the answer, make your best guess**. Unless you've been told that there is a penalty for guessing, choose the answer that you think is likeliest to be correct.

5. **Keep track of the time.** Answering all the questions on a test usually results in a better score. That's why finishing the test is important. Keep track of the time you have left. At the beginning of the test, figure out how many questions you will have to answer by the halfway point in order to finish in the time given.

☑ **Reading Check** What are at least two good ways to avoid skipping lines on an answer sheet?

Understand Types of Test Questions

Most tests include two types of questions: multiple choice and open-ended. Specific strategies will help you understand and correctly answer each type of question.

A **multiple-choice question** has two parts. The first part is the question itself, called the stem. The second part is a series of possible answers. Usually four possible answers are provided, and only one of them is correct. Your task is to choose the correct answer. Here are some strategies to help you do just that.

1. Read and think about each question carefully before looking at the possible answers.

2. Pay close attention to key words in the question. For example, look for the word *not*, as in "Which of the following is not a cause of the conflict in this story?"

3. Read and think about all of the possible answers before making your choice.

4. Reduce the number of choices by eliminating any answers you know are incorrect. Then, think about why some of the remaining choices might also be incorrect.

   • If two of the choices are pretty much the same, both are probably wrong.

   • Answers that contain any of the following words are usually incorrect: *always, never, none, all,* and *only.*

5. If you're still unsure about an answer, see if any of the following applies:

   • When one choice is longer and more detailed than the others, it is often the correct answer.

   • When a choice repeats a word that is in the question, it may be the correct answer.

   • When two choices are direct opposites, one of them is likely the correct answer.

   • When one choice includes one or more of the other choices, it is often the correct answer.

   • When a choice includes the word *some* or *often*, it may be the correct answer.

   • If one of the choices is *All of the above,* make sure that at least two of the other choices seem correct.

   • If one of the choices is *None of the above,* make sure that none of the other choices seems correct.

☑ **Reading Check** What words in a multiple-choice question probably signal a wrong answer?

An **open-ended test item** can take many forms. It might ask you to write a word or phrase to complete a sentence. You might be asked to create a chart, draw a map, or fill in a graphic organizer. Sometimes, you will be asked to write one or more paragraphs in response to a writing prompt. Use the following strategies when reading and answering open-ended items:

1. If the item includes directions, read them carefully. Take note of any steps required.

2. Look for key words and phrases in the item as you plan how you will respond. Does the item ask you to identify a cause-and-effect relationship or to compare and contrast two or more things? Are you supposed to provide a sequence of events or make a generalization? Does the item ask you to write an essay in which you state your point of view and then try to persuade others that your view is correct?

3. If you're going to be writing a paragraph or more, plan your answer. Jot down notes and a brief outline of what you want to say before you begin writing.

4. Focus your answer. Don't include everything you can think of, but be sure to include everything the item asks for.

5. If you're creating a chart or drawing a map, make sure your work is as clear as possible.

☑ **Reading Check** What are at least three key strategies for answering an open-ended question?

READING STRATEGIES
FOR ASSESSMENT

Find the author's main idea.
Think about the focus of the
article. What has the author set
out to do?

Reading Test Model
LONG SELECTIONS

DIRECTIONS Following is an excerpt from an article
entitled "The Empire of the Aztecs." Read the excerpt
carefully. The notes in the side columns will help you
prepare for the types of questions that are likely to
follow a reading like this. You might want to preview the
questions on pages 166–167 before you begin reading.

from The Empire of the Aztecs

When the Spanish explorer Hernán Cortés
marched into the Aztec capital of Tenochtitlán
in 1519, he was amazed at what he found.
Tenochtitlán, the site of present-day Mexico
City, was built on two islands in the middle
of Lake Texcoco. Tenochtitlán was connected
to the mainland by causeways, or raised
earthen roads. The city was much larger and
more populous than any city in Spain. The
people enjoyed a sophisticated lifestyle fueled
by a prosperous economy. In fact, life in the
Aztec empire five hundred years ago was
remarkably similar to life in Mexico today.

Family Life The family was at the
center of Aztec society. An Aztec family
usually consisted of a husband and wife,
their unmarried children, and some of the
husband's relatives. Everyone had a role to
play that contributed to the family's well-
being. The husband supported the family by
farming or working at a craft. His wife tended
to the home. She cooked and wove cloth,
which she used to make the family's clothing.
Each family belonged to a larger social group

called a *calpolli*. The *calpolli* was made up of closely related families who shared farmland. Its structure was similar to a small village.

Boys were taught by their fathers until around age 10. Then they attended schools established by their *calpolli*, where they received a general education and military training. Some children, especially the children of noble families, attended temple schools. There they received the religious training necessary to become priests or community leaders.

Housing The type of house an Aztec family occupied depended on where the family lived. At higher elevations, the climate required houses made of adobe, a mixture of sun-dried earth and straw. In the lowlands, where the climate was milder, houses were constructed with branches or reeds cemented together with clay. They were then topped with thatched roofs. Most homes consisted of several buildings: the main dwelling where the family lived and worked, a sweathouse for taking steam baths, and a storehouse.

Clothing In Aztec society, most people wore similar types of clothing. Men wore a piece of cloth that encircled their hips and a cape that was knotted over one shoulder. Women wore a wraparound skirt topped by a loose, sleeveless blouse.

Draw conclusions How are Aztec families similar to families today? How are they different?

Notice topic sentences. A topic sentence reveals the purpose of a paragraph by telling you what the paragraph is about.

As in many societies today, clothing was an indicator of social and economic status. The clothing most ordinary Aztecs wore was woven from the coarse fibers of the maguey plant. Nobles, however, enjoyed clothing made from soft cotton cloth. In addition, their clothing was often decorated with feathers and other ornaments to signal their status in society.

Diet The Aztecs dined on meat and vegetables, and some of their dishes remain popular to this day. Hunters brought home ducks, geese, rabbits, and deer. The farms of the *calpolli* provided corn, avocados, squashes, papayas, sweet potatoes, beans, and tomatoes.

A staple of the Aztec diet was the *tlaxcalli*, a thin pancake made from corn. We know it today by its Spanish name—*tortilla*. *Tlaxcallis* often were used to scoop up other foods. When the Aztecs wrapped *tlaxcallis* around bits of meat or vegetables, they called the result *tacos*.

The favorite beverage of the Aztecs was a drink made from chocolate. Because chocolate was made from expensive cacao beans, only wealthy nobles could enjoy it regularly.

Economy As in modern societies, the success of the Aztec empire was largely due to its economy. The Aztec economy was based on agriculture. In addition to fruits and

Pay attention to foreign words and phrases. Foreign words and phrases will appear in italic type. Each word or phrase will be defined the first time it is used.

Observe comparisons. How is the success of the Aztec society like the success of modern societies?

vegetables, the Aztecs grew cotton and cacao beans and harvested latex to make rubber.

Aztec agricultural methods were similar to methods still in use today. In heavily forested areas, farmers used a technique called "slash-and-burn." They would cut down the trees and burn them, making a clearing in which crops could be planted. Where the landscape was hilly, farmers cut terraces into the hills. These terraces greatly increased the acreage of level land that could be farmed. In wetland areas, farmers created islands, called *chinampas*, by scooping and piling up the fertile mud of the wetland.

The bounty from the Aztec farmlands, along with the works of artists and craftspeople, found its way to marketplaces throughout the empire. The largest market anywhere in the Americas was in the city of Tlatelolco. Cortés himself estimated that this market attracted over 60,000 traders each day. The Aztecs traded because they had no money in the modern sense of that word. Instead, they offered one type of good in exchange for another type—cacao beans for a richly decorated blouse, for example, or a jaguar pelt for brightly colored bird feathers.

Language The language the Aztec spoke, *Nahuatl*, belonged to a family of languages called Aztec-Tanoan. This language family included languages spoken by Native

Notice supporting details. What three types of farming methods did the Aztecs use? Where did they use each type?

Think about the author's purpose. Is this article meant to inform, persuade, entertain, or describe?

Americans, including the Comanche and the Shoshone.

The Aztecs had a written language, but it was based on pictures, not unlike the hieroglyphs of ancient Egypt. Each picture represented either an idea or the sound of a *Nahuatl* syllable. Because their written language was limited, the Aztecs used it mainly for government and religious purposes.

The Arts Artistic expression was important to the Aztecs. They created monumental sculptures to decorate their temples and other important buildings. Craft workers produced beautiful metalware, pottery, wood carvings, and weavings.

The Aztecs valued music and literature as well. Flutes, rattles, and drums provided a musical background for religious ceremonies. Poetry and historical accounts were handed down orally through the generations.

Religion The central focus of Aztec life was religion, and this is where Aztec society differed greatly from societies today. Hundreds of Aztec gods and goddesses presided over every aspect of human life: farming, the weather, war, fertility, the sun, the wind, and fire, to name just a few. In addition to a 365-day solar calendar, the Aztecs also had a 260-day religious calendar. This calendar helped Aztec priests decide the best time of the year to plant crops, go to war, or build new temples.

The Aztec gods demanded a great deal of attention from their followers. To appease their gods, the Aztecs held many religious ceremonies. The centerpiece of these ceremonies was human sacrifice. The Aztecs believed that the gods drew strength and bravery from the blood of sacrificial victims. Most of the victims were slaves or prisoners of war. In fact, the Aztecs sometimes went to war just to get prisoners for their religious ceremonies.

ANSWER STRATEGIES

Understand the meaning of *purpose*. An author's purpose is his or her reason for writing. Just because a selection is entertaining doesn't necessarily mean entertainment was the author's reason for writing.

1 Which of the following best describes the author's purpose?

A. to entertain

B. to inform

C. to describe

D. to persuade

Read foreign words and phrases carefully. This excerpt uses many foreign words and phrases. Be sure you locate the one asked for in the question before you choose an answer.

2 What is a *tlaxcalli*?

A. a thin corn pancake

B. a drink made from cacao

C. a *tortilla* wrapped around meat or vegetables

D. a social group

Find main ideas. Remember that the main idea of a piece of writing describes what the author will talk about throughout the *entire* selection and not just one part of it.

3 Which of the following best expresses the author's main idea?

A. Hernán Cortés was amazed when he first saw the Aztec city of Tenochtitlán.

B. The Aztecs enjoyed a sophisticated lifestyle.

C. Life in the Aztec empire was similar in many ways to life today.

D. The family was at the center of Aztec society.

4 Which of the following is NOT a conclusion you can draw about how Aztec and modern families are alike?

   A. Children went to school for their education.

   B. Parents provided for their families.

   C. Families are part of larger social groups.

   D. Relatives of the husband live with the husband's family.

> **Note key words.** Pay attention to the key word or words in the question. The key word here is *not*.

5 Which method of farming involved clearing the forest?

   A. slash-and-burn

   B. crop rotation

   C. cutting terraces

   D. creating islands

> **Don't rely on memory.** Each of the responses to this question is a type of farming. One of them, however, is never mentioned in the excerpt. Before answering, look back at the excerpt and find the types that *are* mentioned.

6 In what ways is the Aztec religion similar to and different from modern religions?

> **Plan your response.** Read the question carefully. This question asks you to compare and contrast. Look for similarities and differences and state them in your own words.

Sample short response for question 6:

The Aztec religion shares many similarities with modern religions. The Aztecs recognized the existence of gods. They believed these gods would protect them if they respected and worshipped the gods. Also, the Aztecs held regular religious services and ceremonies. The most important difference between the Aztec religion and modern religions is human sacrifice. Today, people pray to their god or gods and make offerings, but no religions practice human sacrifice.

> **Study your response.** Notice how the writer follows the same organization as the question—similarities first and then differences.

Reading Test Practice
LONG SELECTIONS

DIRECTIONS Now it's time to practice what you've learned about reading test items and choosing the best answers. Read the following selection, "The Gauchos of the Pampa." Use the side columns to make notes about the important parts of this selection: the setting, important ideas, comparisons and contrasts, difficult vocabulary, interesting details, and so on.

The Gauchos of the Pampa

In the mythology of Argentina, no one sits taller in the saddle than the gauchos. Part expert horsemen and part outlaws, these free spirits of the Pampas played a brief but crucial role in the development of cattle ranching and agriculture in Argentina. Although the gaucho era lasted barely a century, it remains an essential part of Argentina's culture, celebrated in literature and song.

La Pampa Stretching across central Argentina from the Atlantic coast to the foothills of the Andes, *la Pampa*, the Pampa, is a nearly flat plain. It is bordered to the north by the Gran Chaco and to the south by Patagonia. The Quechuas gave the Pampa its name. In their language it means "flat surface." Today, the region is commonly known as "the Pampas." It was onto this great plain that the Spanish introduced both cattle and horses. Soon, great herds of these animals were running wild throughout the eastern Pampas.

The Rise of the Gauchos Portuguese, Dutch, British, and French traders were eager to exploit the resources provided by the herds, namely hides and tallow, a waxy white fat used to make soap and candles. In turn, the horsemen of the Pampas were eager to help the traders because cattle and horse rustling was a profitable, if illegal, business. Thus were born the gauchos, who soon established their own culture on the plains of Argentina.

The gauchos lived simply, in mud huts with thatched roofs, sleeping on piles of hides. They formed families and had children, but their marriages were rarely officially recognized by the state or the church. Favorite pastimes of the gauchos included horseback riding and guitar playing.

Tools of the Gaucho Trade Everything about the gaucho lifestyle was geared to existence on the plains, including their clothing. Typically, a gaucho wore long, accordion-pleated trousers called *bombachas* that were tucked securely into high leather boots. A wide silver belt was cinched at the waist. A warm woolen poncho and a brightly colored scarf completed the costume.

The gaucho's weapons were simple and effective: a lasso, a sharp knife, and, most importantly, a *boleadora*, or *bola*. The bola consisted of three long leather cords attached at one end. At the other end of each cord was a stone or iron ball. Galloping after a stampeding herd of horses or cattle, the gaucho would twirl the bola in the air and then release it, parallel to the ground, at the legs of a fleeing animal. The bola would wrap itself around the animal's legs and send it crashing to the ground.

The End of an Era Toward the end of the 18th century, many of the gauchos had become legitimate animal handlers. They were hired by businessmen who had acquired large herds of wild cattle and horses. Then, during the 19th century, large tracts of the Pampas were carved into vast ranches called *estancias* or estates. The wild animals of the Pampas were slowly replaced with purebred stock from Europe. Railroads were built across the Pampas to transport livestock and tractors replaced horses on the ranches. The gaucho lifestyle had come to an end, and the remaining gauchos were now *peones*, or farmhands.

Celebrating the Gaucho Although the gaucho lifestyle ended, the gaucho legend lives on. During the heyday of the gaucho, a rich literary tradition had begun chronicling their exploits. In 1872, José Hernández wrote his epic poem *El gaucho Martín Fierro (The Gaucho Martin Fierro)*. Fifteen years later, the celebrated gaucho minstrel Santos Vega was the subject of three poems by Rafael Obligado. As late as 1926, Argentinian writer Ricardo Güiraldes added to the body of gaucho literature with *Don Segundo Sombra: Shadows in the Pampas*.

Like the age of the American cowboy, the gaucho era was a colorful time in the history of the Pampas. Even today, the legend and spirit

of the gaucho is kept alive through traveling
gaucho shows, reminders of a time when the
Pampas and the proud, independent people
who lived there shaped the future of Argentina.

Now answer questions 1–7. Base your answers on the selection "The Gauchos of the Pampa."

1 Which of the following best describes the main idea of this selection?

   A. The gauchos were free spirits.

   B. The gauchos played a crucial role in the development of cattle ranching and agriculture.

   C. The gaucho era lasted barely a century.

   D. The gauchos were expert horsemen and outlaws.

2 Patagonia lies in which direction from the Pampas?

   A. north

   B. west

   C. east

   D. south

3 Why did the gauchos agree to help the European traders?

   A. Cattle rustling was illegal.

   B. Cattle rustling was profitable.

   C. Cattle rustling was an outlaw's trade.

   D. Cattle rustling was not profitable.

4 Which of the following does NOT describe the gaucho lifestyle?

   A. The gauchos lived on large ranches.

   B. The gauchos lived in mud huts.

   C. The gauchos enjoyed playing the guitar.

   D. The gauchos slept on piles of hides.

5 Why was the bola an effective weapon?

   A. It had long leather cords attached at one end.

   B. It was easy to twirl and throw.

   C. It had three heavy stone or iron balls.

   D. It tripped the animal being hunted so the animal could no longer run.

6 Why does the author describe the gauchos as "proud, independent people"?

   A. because they were outlaws

   B. because they endured harsh conditions on the Pampas

   C. because they made a living successfully by their own rules

   D. because they agreed to work for others

7 Explain why the era of the gauchos came to an end.

THINKING IT THROUGH

The notes in the side columns will help you think through your answers. See the answer key at the bottom of the next page. How well did you do?

Each answer lists a detail from the opening paragraph. However, since the main idea tells about the focus of the *entire* selection, you can easily eliminate three of the four choices.

1 Which of the following best describes the main idea of this selection?

   A. The gauchos were free spirits.

   B. The gauchos played a crucial role in the development of cattle ranching and agriculture.

   C. The gaucho era lasted barely a century.

   D. The gauchos were expert horsemen and outlaws.

Skim the reading looking for the key word *Patagonia*.

2 Patagonia lies in which direction from the Pampas?

   A. north

   B. west

   C. east

   D. south

Notice that answer choices A and C say the same thing. Answer choices B and D are opposites—a good clue that either B or D is the correct answer.

3 Why did the gauchos agree to help the European traders?

   A. Cattle rustling was illegal.

   B. Cattle rustling was profitable.

   C. Cattle rustling was an outlaw's trade.

   D. Cattle rustling was not profitable.

Read the question carefully. A word printed in capital letters is important to understanding the question correctly.

4 Which of the following does NOT describe the gaucho lifestyle?

   A. The gauchos lived on large ranches.

   B. The gauchos lived in mud huts.

   C. The gauchos enjoyed playing the guitar.

   D. The gauchos slept on piles of hides.

5 Why was the bola an effective weapon?

   A. It had long leather cords attached at one end.

   B. It was easy to twirl and throw.

   C. It had three heavy stone or iron balls.

   D. It tripped the animal being hunted so the animal could no longer run.

> Notice that the first three choices just describe properties of the bola. Only the last choice describes how the bola worked to bring down prey.

6 Why does the author describe the gauchos as "proud, independent people"?

   A. because they were outlaws

   B. because they endured harsh conditions on the Pampas

   C. because they made a living successfully by their own rules

   D. because they agreed to work for others

> This question asks you to infer meaning. What do "proud" and "independent" mean? Which answer choice reflects the meaning of the two words?

7 Explain why the era of the gauchos came to an end.

The gaucho era came to an end because Argentina was changing. First, the once wild herds were acquired by people who wanted to manage them and profit from them. The gauchos were hired by these people. Then, the Pampas was "carved into vast ranches." These ranches meant that the gauchos could no longer roam freely. Railroads were built to transport the cattle, making cattle drives unnecessary. Soon, the only way the gauchos could make a living was to work as farmhands.

> This is considered a strong response because it
> - directly addresses the question and stays focused on the topic.
> - uses supporting details from the selection, including a quotation, to make its point.
> - is written clearly, using correct spelling, grammar, and punctuation.

READING STRATEGIES FOR ASSESSMENT

Find the main idea and supporting details. Circle the main idea of this article. Then underline the details that support the main idea.

Use context clues. To discover what a "pack animal" is, study the words and phrases around it. Which phrase helps define it?

Notice important details. Underline the details that explain why alpaca wool is so desirable.

Reading Test Model
SHORT SELECTIONS

DIRECTIONS "Warmth from the Andes" is a short informative article. The strategies you have just learned can also help you with this shorter selection. As you read the selection, respond to the notes in the side column.

When you've finished reading, answer the multiple-choice questions. Use the side-column notes to help you understand what each question is asking and why each answer is correct.

Warmth from the Andes

Southeastern Peru and Western Bolivia make up a geographic region called the *Altiplano*, or High Plateau. This largely desolate mountainous area is home to one of the most economically important animals in South America—the alpaca.

The alpaca is related to the camel and looks somewhat like another well-known South American grazing animal, the llama. Alpacas live at elevations as high as 16,000 feet. At such altitudes, oxygen is scarce. Alpacas are able to survive because their blood contains an unusually high number of red blood corpuscles, the cells that carry oxygen throughout the body.

For several thousand years, the Native Americans of the region have raised alpacas both as pack animals for transporting goods and for their most important resource—wool. Alpaca wool ranges in color from black to tan to white. It is lightweight yet strong and resists moisture. Also, it is exceptionally warm. Alpaca wool is much finer than the wool from sheep. In fact, it is so luxurious that when the Inca civilization dominated the *Altiplano* region, garments made from Alpaca wool could be worn only by royalty.

Alpacas are usually sheared once each year by herders in Bolivia and Peru. Some of the wool is sold to manufacturers in the United States and Europe to be woven into cloth as soft and sought after as cashmere. The herders sell the rest to local weavers, who use it to produce beautiful shawls and other fine garments.

1 Which of the following best describes the main idea of the article?

A. Alpacas can survive at high altitudes.

B. The *Altiplano* is a high plateau.

C. The alpaca is related to the camel.

D. The Alpaca is one of the most economically important animals of South America.

Identify the focus. Each answer choice offers information from the article, but only one choice explains what the entire article is about.

2 Which of the following best describes what pack animals do?

A. transport goods

B. survive at high altitudes

C. provide wool for clothing

D. graze on the *Altiplano*

Pay attention to the context of unfamiliar words. Find the sentence in the article where *pack animals* is used. Notice that only one answer choice is a phrase found right next to *pack animals*.

3 Why is alpaca wool highly prized?

A. It resembles the fur of camels.

B. It has been woven for thousands of years.

C. It is lightweight, warm, strong, and resists moisture.

D. It can be worn only by royalty.

Evaluate details. Something "highly prized" has important qualities. Which answer choice talks about the qualities of alpaca wool?

Answers:
1. D, 2. A, 3. C

Read the title. What does the title tell you the chart is about?

_____

_____

Read the labels What do the labels on the left side of the chart tell you? What about the labels at the top of the chart?

ANSWER STRATEGIES

> **Read the question carefully.** Notice that the questions asks for depth in feet, not meters.

> **Read the labels carefully.** Be sure you understand which column represents square miles and which represents square kilometers.

> **Follow rows and columns carefully.** If necessary, use your finger to trace across a row or down a column so that you don't accidentally wind up in the wrong place with the wrong information.

DIRECTIONS Some test questions ask you to analyze a visual rather than a reading selection. Study this chart carefully and answer the questions that follow.

Largest Lakes of Central and South America

	Surface Area (sq. mi./sq. km.)	Depth (feet/meters)	Elevation (feet/meters)
Lake Maracaibo, Venezuela	5,200/13,468	197/60	sea level
Lake Titicaca, Bolivia and Peru	3,200/8,288	990/302	12,500/3,810
Lake Nicaragua, Nicaragua	3,150/8,159	230/70	102/31

④ What is the depth, in feet, of the deepest lake?

A. 990

B. 12,500

C. 302

D. 13,468

⑤ What is the surface area of Lake Titicaca in square kilometers?

A. 3,200

B. 302

C. 8,288

D. 3,810

⑥ At what altitude is Lake Maracaibo?

A. 197 feet

B. sea level

C. 12,500 feet

D. 31 sq. km.

Answers:
4. A, 5. C, 6. B

Reading Test Practice
SHORT SELECTIONS

DIRECTIONS Use the following to practice your skills. Read the paragraphs carefully. Then answer the multiple-choice questions that follow.

During the 1990s, Spanish opera singer Plácido Domingo teamed up with two other singers, Italy's Luciano Pavarotti and Spain's José Carreras, to form a wildly popular singing group known as The Three Tenors. They enjoyed worldwide success, touring and appearing on television. Domingo's musical career, however, got its start much earlier— mid-century, in fact.

Born in Madrid in 1941, Domingo and his parents moved to Mexico City in 1950 where he began studying singing at the National Conservatory of Music. Ten years later, Domingo made his opera debut in a production of *La Traviata* in Monterrey, Mexico. After a three-year stint with the Israeli National Opera, Domingo joined the New York City Opera in 1966. Two years later, he made his debut with the Metropolitan Opera of New York.

Over the next three decades, Domingo dazzled audiences with his technical skill and virtuoso acting. Thirty-six years after his debut in Monterrey, Domingo became the artistic director of the Washington (D.C.) Opera. Then, in 2000, he assumed the same post at the Los Angeles Opera.

1 **What was the author's purpose in writing this selection?**

   A. to persuade readers that Plácido Domingo is a great opera singer

   B. to explain who The Three Tenors were

   C. to inform readers about the career of Plácido Domingo

   D. to describe the roles Plácido Domingo has sung during his career

2 **Which of the following is NOT a conclusion you can draw from the selection?**

   A. Domingo is the greatest opera singer of his generation.

   B. Domingo has had a successful career as an opera singer.

   C. Domingo, Pavarotti, and Carreras captivated audiences with their singing.

   D. Domingo is widely respected in the opera world as a singer and an artist.

DIRECTIONS Use the graph below to answer the questions that follow.

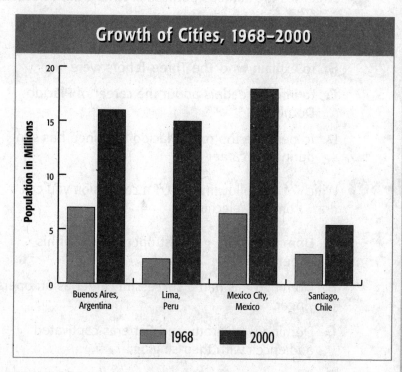

Growth of Cities, 1968–2000

1968   2000

3 Which city had the SMALLEST population in 1968?

A. Lima

B. Buenos Aires

C. Santiago

D. Mexico City

4 Which city had the LARGEST population in 2000?

A. Lima

B. Buenos Aires

C. Santiago

D. Mexico City

5 Which city had the SMALLEST increase in population between 1968 and 2000?

A. Lima

B. Buenos Aires

C. Santiago

D. Mexico City

THINKING IT THROUGH

1 What was the author's purpose in writing this selection?

- **A.** to persuade readers that Plácido Domingo is a great opera singer
- **B.** to explain who The Three Tenors were
- **C.** to inform readers about the career of Plácido Domingo
- **D.** to describe the roles Plácido Domingo has sung during his career

2 Which of the following is NOT a conclusion you can draw from the selection?

- **A.** Domingo is the greatest opera singer of his generation.
- **B.** Domingo has had a successful career as an opera singer.
- **C.** Domingo, Pavarotti, and Carreras captivated audiences with their singing.
- **D.** Domingo is widely respected in the opera world as a singer and an artist.

3 Which city had the SMALLEST population in 1968?

- **A.** Lima
- **B.** Buenos Aires
- **C.** Santiago
- **D.** Mexico City

4 Which city had the LARGEST population in 2000?

- **A.** Lima
- **B.** Buenos Aires
- **C.** Santiago
- **D.** Mexico City

5 Which city had the SMALLEST increase in population between 1968 and 2000?

- **A.** Lima
- **B.** Buenos Aires
- **C.** Santiago
- **D.** Mexico City

Answers:
1. C, 2. A, 3. A, 4. D, 5. C

Functional Reading Test Model

DIRECTIONS Study the following nutrition label from a jar of tomatillo salsa. Then answer the questions that follow.

Nutrition Facts

Serving Size 2 TBSP (30 g)
Servings Per Container 15

Amount Per Serving

Calories 10

Calories from Fat 0

	% Daily Value*
Total Fat 0 g	0%
Saturated Fat 0 g	0%
Cholesterol 0 mg	0%
Sodium 230 mg	10%
Total Carbohydrate 2 g	
Dietary Fiber 0 g	0%
Sugars 1 g	
Protein 0 g	

Vitamin A 6% • Vitamin C 8%

Calcium 4% • Iron 0%

* Percent Daily Values are based on a 2,000 calorie diet.

1 How many calories does this whole bottle of salsa contain?

A. 10

B. 150

C. 15

D. 30

2 If you ate two servings of salsa, how many mg. of sodium would you consume?

A. 460

B. 10

C. 230

D. 690

3 Is salsa a smart food choice for people trying to limit their fat intake?

A. No, because it has 230 mg of sodium per serving.

B. Yes, because the serving size is just 2 TBSP.

C. No, because it has ten calories per serving.

D. Yes, because each serving has 0 g of fat.

READING STRATEGIES FOR ASSESSMENT

Examine the structure of the label. Notice the type of information included in each of the four parts of the label.

Do the math. Remember that the "% Daily Value" and vitamin and mineral numbers on the label are for just a single serving.

ANSWER STRATEGIES

To find the correct answer, multiply the number of calories per serving by the number of servings in the bottle.

Again, multiplication is the key to finding the correct answer.

To answer this question, just look at that part of the label that tells how much fat each serving contains.

Answers:
1. B, 2. A, 3. D

Functional Reading Test Practice

DIRECTIONS Study the following travel advertisement for a vacation package to Puerto Rico. Circle the information that you think is the most important. Then answer the multiple-choice questions that follow.

EXPERIENCE THE EXCITEMENT OF PUERTO RICO!

Snorkeling! Windsurfing! Sailing! Golf! First-Class Entertainment!

4 days/3 nights at the San Juan Adventure Resort

only $479 per person
airfare included *

Adventure Resort Package also includes continental breakfast, two beach passes, two spa treatments

* Price based on double occupancy. Airfare from New York City only. From Chicago add $175. From Los Angeles add $350. Single travelers add $200.

---

1. Which of the following is NOT included in the $479 price?

   A. beach passes

   B. windsurfing

   C. spa treatments

   D. continental breakfast

2. How much will this vacation package cost a single traveler from Los Angeles?

   A. $479

   B. $654

   C. $679

   D. $1,029

3. For which of the following is this vacation package the LEAST expensive per person?

   A. two sisters from New York

   B. a stockbroker from Los Angeles

   C. a single traveler from New York

   D. a college student from Chicago

THINKING IT THROUGH

The notes in the side column will help you think through your answers. Check the answer key at the bottom of the page. How well did you do?

> Although the ad mentions windsurfing prominently, it does not indicate that this activity is included in the price.

1 Which of the following is NOT included in the $479 price?

   A. beach passes

   B. windsurfing

   C. spa treatments

   D. continental breakfast

> To answer this question, read the small type at the bottom of the ad and add the extra charges to the advertised price.

2 How much will this vacation package cost a single traveler from Los Angeles?

   A. $479

   B. $654

   C. $679

   D. $1,029

> Read each answer choice carefully. How many people are traveling? Where are they coming from? Then use the information in the ad to determine who will get the best deal.

3 For which of the following travelers is this vacation package the LEAST expensive per person?

   A. two sisters from New York

   B. a stockbroker from Los Angeles

   C. a single traveler from New York

   D. a college student from Chicago

Revising-and-Editing Test Model

DIRECTIONS Read the following paragraph carefully. Then answer the multiple-choice questions that follow. After answering the questions, read the material in the side columns to check your answer strategies.

¹Madrid, the capital of Spain. ²It is home to one of that nations cultural treasures—the Prado museum. ³The building was constructed in the late eighteenth century as a museum of natural science. ⁴Then they decided to change it to an art museum in 1819 and it has more than 9,000 works of art. ⁵The museum is located on a street called the Paseo del Prado. ⁶Their are many famous paintings they're, including works by El Greco, Velázquez, and Goya.

① Which sentence in the paragraph is actually a fragment, an incomplete thought?

   A. sentence 5

   B. sentence 3

   C. sentence 1

   D. sentence 4

② In sentence 2, which of the following is the correct possessive form of *nation*?

   A. nation's

   B. nations's

   C. nations'

   D. nations

READING STRATEGIES FOR ASSESSMENT

Watch for common errors. Highlight or underline errors such as incorrect spelling or punctuation; fragments or run-on sentences; and missing or misplaced information.

ANSWER STRATEGIES

Incomplete sentences. A sentence is a group of words with a subject and a verb that expresses a complete thought. If either the subject or the verb is missing, the group of words is an incomplete sentence.

Possessive nouns. In sentence 2, the word *nation* is singular. So, it takes the singular possessive form.

Pronoun references. Avoid unclear or inaccurate pronoun references. In sentence 4, *they* has no antecedent at all and so must be replaced with the noun *government*. The antecedent for *it* is unclear and must be replaced with *the natural science museum*.

Run-on sentences. A run-on sentence is two or more complete thoughts joined without correct punctuation. Often the word *and* is used instead of a period to connect the two complete thoughts—a clue that the sentence is a run-on.

Spelling errors. Words that sound the same may be spelled differently and have different meanings. Check to be sure that the spelling you use carries the meaning you intend.

Logical organization. The order of the sentences in a paragraph should be logical. The location of the Prado logically should come before the sentence that discusses the museum's construction.

3 What is the best way to rewrite the first part of sentence 4?

  A. Then he decided to change it to an art museum

  B. Then the government decided to change it to an art museum

  C. Then the government decided to change the natural science museum to an art museum

  D. Then he decided to change the natural science museum to an art museum

4 Which sentence in the paragraph is a run-on sentence?

  A. sentence 2

  B. sentence 5

  C. sentence 1

  D. sentence 4

5 What is the best way to rewrite the first part of sentence 6?

  A. They're many famous paintings their

  B. There are many famous paintings they're

  C. There are many famous paintings there

  D. Their are many famous paintings there

6 Sentence 5 is out of place. Where should sentence 5 occur?

  A. after sentence 2

  B. before sentence 2

  C. after sentence 5

  D. after sentence 3

Revising-and-Editing Test Practice

DIRECTIONS Read the following paragraph carefully. As you read, circle each error that you find and identify the error in the side column—for example, *misspelled word* or *incorrect punctuation*. When you have finished, circle the letter of the correct choice for each question that follows.

¹On December, 17, 1830, one of the most greatest leaders in South American history died. ²He was born in Venezuela, which was ruled by Spain. ³As a young man, Simón Bolívar tours Europe, and he vows to free Venezuela from Spanish rule. ⁴After a series of setbacks. ⁵Bolívar began winning his fight to oust the Spanish from South America. ⁶By 1824, Spanish rule in South America was over and Bolívar is now known as *El Libertador* and the "George Washington of South America."

1 Which sentence in the paragraph is a fragment?

   A. sentence 4

   B. sentence 2

   C. sentence 6

   D. sentence 7

2 What is the correct way to write the date in sentence 1?

   A. Dec./17/1830

   B. December 17 1830

   C. December 17, 1830

   D. December, 17 1830

3 In sentence 1, which of the following is the correct form of the superlative adjective?

A. greatest

B. greater

C. more great

D. more greatest

4 Which of the following errors occurs in sentence 2?

A. unclear pronoun reference

B. incorrect capitalization

C. incorrect punctuation

D. incorrect verb tense

5 Which of the following is the correct way to rewrite the first part of sentence 3?

A. As a young man, Simón Bolívar tours Europe, and he vowed

B. As a young man, Simón Bolívar toured Europe, and he vows

C. As a young man, Simón Bolívar is touring Europe, and he vows

D. As a young man, Simón Bolívar toured Europe, and he vowed

6 Which of the following is the best way to punctuate the middle of sentence 6?

A. Spanish rule in South America was over: and Bolívar is now

B. Spanish rule in South America was over. Bolívar is now

C. Spanish rule in South America was over; and Bolívar is now

D. Spanish rule in South America was over—and Bolívar is now

THINKING IT THROUGH

Use the notes in the side columns to help you understand why some answers are correct and others are not. Check the answer key on the next page. How well did you do?

1 Which sentence in the paragraph is a fragment?

   A. sentence 4

   B. sentence 2

   C. sentence 6

   D. sentence 7

> Remember that a sentence has a subject and a verb and expresses a complete thought. Which sentence is lacking either a subject or a verb?

2 What is the correct way to write the date in sentence 1?

   A. Dec./17/1830

   B. December 17 1830

   C. December 17, 1830

   D. December, 17 1830

> When writing a date, the name of the month should be spelled out, and the day and year should be separated by a comma.

3 In sentence 1, which of the following is the correct form of the superlative adjective?

   A. greatest

   B. greater

   C. more great

   D. more greatest

> A superlative adjective is formed by adding -est to the adjective or placing the word *most* before the adjective. Never do both at the same time.

First check to be sure that words are capitalized correctly, that the sentence is punctuated correctly, and that the verb has the same tense as other verbs in the paragraph. Then ask, "Who is *he*?" Unless you can answer that question with a proper name, the pronoun reference is unclear.

Remember that all the verbs in a paragraph should agree: that is, have the same tense. So both verbs in sentence 3 must agree.

Remember that a run-on sentence is two or more sentences strung together with either no punctuation or incorrect punctuation. The solution is to create separate sentences.

④ Which of the following errors occurs in sentence 2?

A. unclear pronoun reference

B. incorrect capitalization

C. incorrect punctuation

D. incorrect verb tense

⑤ Which of the following is the correct way to rewrite the first part of sentence 3?

A. As a young man, Simón Bolívar tours Europe, and he vowed

B. As a young man, Simón Bolívar toured Europe, and he vows

C. As a young man, Simón Bolívar is touring Europe, and he vows

D. As a young man, Simón Bolívar toured Europe, and he vowed

⑥ Which of the following is the best way to punctuate the middle of sentence 6?

A. Spanish rule in South America was over: and Bolívar is now

B. Spanish rule in South America was over. Bolívar is now

C. Spanish rule in South America was over; and Bolívar is now

D. Spanish rule in South America was over—and Bolívar is now

Writing Test Model

DIRECTIONS Many tests ask you to write an essay in response to a writing prompt. A writing prompt is a brief statement that describes a writing situation. Some writing prompts ask you to explain *what, why,* or *how.* Others ask you to convince someone of something.

As you analyze the following writing prompts, read and respond to the notes in the side columns. Then look at the response to each prompt. The notes in the side columns will help you understand why each response is considered strong.

Prompt A

Some child-rearing experts believe that young people should be kept busy after school and on the weekends with a variety of structured activities, such as music lessons, sports, dance classes, and so on. Others say that young people today have been "overscheduled" and need more time to themselves—to read, think about the future, and even just to daydream.

Think about your experiences and the way your non-school time is structured. Do you think lots of structure, more personal time, or a combination of the two is most beneficial to young people? Remember to provide solid reasons and examples for the position you take.

ANALYZING THE PROMPT

Identify the focus. What issue will you be writing about? Circle the focus of your essay in the first sentence of the prompt.

Understand what's expected of you. First, circle what the prompt asks you to do. Then identify your audience. What kinds of details will appeal to this audience?

Strong Response

Today was a typical day for my little brother Jeff. He got up at five o'clock to go to the local ice rink for hockey practice. Then he was off to school. At the end of the school day,

ANSWER STRATEGIES

Capture the reader's interest. The writer begins by describing a typical busy day in his younger brother's life.

Jeff had a piano lesson followed by a meeting of his Cub Scout troop. After a quick dinner, he did homework for two hours. He finally got to bed at ten o'clock. That's a lot to pack into a single day, especially since Jeff is just seven years old! I think that in addition to sports, music, and other activities, kids like Jeff need some time to themselves.

Many parents, mine included, think a busy kid is a safe kid. They believe that the less time a kid has on his hands, the less likely he'll wind up doing something he shouldn't be doing or being with people he shouldn't be with. That's probably true for many kids. After all, it's hard to get into trouble when you spend every day being carpooled from one activity to another.

But some busy kids do get into trouble anyway. Jeff's friend Mark got caught trying to shoplift a CD last weekend, and he's involved in just as many activities as Jeff is. So having a busy schedule is no guarantee that a kid won't get into trouble.

Plus, I think kids benefit from having free time to go to the movies, play video games, read, or even just be by themselves. Growing up isn't always easy, and kids need some time alone to figure things out, think about what's important to them, and decide what they really want to do.

Last Saturday afternoon, Jeff's soccer practice was canceled because of thunderstorms. We went to see a movie and later spent some time talking and listening to music in my room. It was the first time in months that we had time just to hang out together, and we really enjoyed it. Jeff said it was like having a day off. I think more kids like Jeff could use a day off too.

State the position clearly. The last sentence of the first paragraph makes the writer's position clear to the reader. Now the writer can spend the rest of the essay developing his argument.

Address opposing views. The writer brings up an opposing view—that busy kids are less likely to get into trouble—and admits that it might sometimes be true.

Use good examples to support the position. Here, the writer uses an example to make the point that not all busy kids stay out of trouble.

Use logical reasoning to further develop the position. The writer offers logical reasons why free time is important.

Restate the position in the conclusion. Using another concrete example, the writer restates his position that kids need some time to themselves.

Prompt B

Depending on where you live, each season of the year can be very different than it is in other parts of the country. Which season do you enjoy the most—summer, autumn, winter, or spring? What is that season like in your part of the country? What makes it special to you?

Strong Response

Here in the upper Midwest, the seasons seem as different from one another as night and day. Summer usually arrives suddenly. The temperatures soar, the humidity rises, and fierce thunderstorms add drama and sometimes destruction to the season. Autumn brings a crisp, cool, and colorful change as the leaves turn golden and the air turns chilly. Winter can be bitterly cold, and heavy snows often make the simple trip to school a real ordeal.

Then comes spring. Spring is a truly magical time of the year. I can sense spring long before it actually arrives. There's a certain scent in the air, and something is different about the way the sunlight looks. Soon the winter snows are reduced to muddy puddles. The tree branches swell with buds, and the first green shoots of crocus and tulip leaves struggle up out of the ground. Most magical of all, the early morning hours just after dawn are filled with the cries of migrating birds heading back north.

Because my family lives in a small community surrounded by farmland, I get to experience a different kind of spring than many people do. The fields behind our house fill up with wildflowers that season the air with perfume and color. A trip to Jefferson's Pond offers a chance to watch ducks and geese resting on their long

ANALYZING THE PROMPT

Look for the main idea. The first few sentences of the prompt present the subject you will write about. Try restating the subject in your own words.

Understand what's expected of you. What does the prompt ask you to do? Explain something? Persuade someone? State your personal feelings?

ANSWER STRATEGIES

Create an intriguing introduction. The writer arouses the reader's curiosity by leaving out one of the four seasons.

Include specific details. The writer uses specific details about each season to make the description vivid.

Include the kind of information the prompt asks for. Notice how the writer follows the directions in the prompt by explaining what spring is like in her part of the country.

Use sensory details. Details that appeal to the reader's sense of sight, sound, and smell bring the description to life.

Make comparisons. Comparing the blossoming trees to balls of cotton candy helps the reader experience the scene as the writer does.

Write a powerful conclusion. The writer ends the essay by comparing herself to her favorite season.

seasonal journeys. The apple and cherry trees at the McKlintock family orchards explode with blossoms until they look like giant balls of cotton candy.

Mostly, however, I love spring because it is a season of hope. The earth is coming back to life, filled with possibilities. I feel like I am, too.

Writing Test Practice

DIRECTIONS Read the following writing prompt. Using the strategies you've learned in this section, analyze the prompt, plan your response, and then write an essay explaining your position.

Prompt C

You have volunteered to participate in your community's semiannual blood drive. Your task is to write a letter to your community newspaper encouraging everyone in town to consider giving blood.

Think about all the ways your community benefits from having an adequate blood supply. Write a letter that explains what these benefits are. Include specific examples. End your letter by appealing to your fellow citizens' sense of civic pride and duty.

Scoring Rubrics

DIRECTIONS Use the following checklist to see whether you have written a strong persuasive essay. You will have succeeded if you can check nearly all of the items.

The Prompt

☐ My response meets all the requirements stated in the prompt.

☐ I have stated my position clearly and supported it with details.

☐ I have addressed the audience appropriately.

☐ My essay fits the type of writing suggested in the prompt (letter to the editor, article for the school paper, and so on).

Reasons

☐ The reasons I offer really support my position.

☐ My audience will find the reasons convincing.

☐ I have stated my reasons clearly.

☐ I have given at least three reasons.

☐ I have supported my reasons with sufficient facts, examples, quotations, and other details.

☐ I have presented and responded to opposing arguments.

☐ My reasoning is sound. I have avoided faulty logic.

Order and Arrangement

☐ I have included a strong introduction.

☐ I have included a strong conclusion.

☐ The reasons are arranged in a logical order.

Word Choice

☐ The language of my essay is appropriate for my audience.

☐ I have used precise, vivid words and persuasive language.

Fluency

☐ I have used sentences of varying lengths and structures.

☐ I have connected ideas with transitions and other devices.

☐ I have used correct spelling, punctuation, and grammar.

Apuntes

Apuntes

Apuntes

Apuntes

Credits

Illustrations

All illustrations by McDougal Littell/Houghton Mifflin Co.

Photography

3, 4 Guy Jarvis/School Division/Houghton Mifflin Co.; **8** Phil Schermeister/Corbis; **9** Royalty-Free/ Corbis; *inset* Carl Schneider/Corbis; **13, 14** The American School Foundation of Guadalajara, A.C.; **18** *bottom* Robert Fried/Alamy; *top* Guy Jarvis/School Division/Houghton Mifflin Co.; **19** *bottom* Robert Frerck/Odyssey Productions, Inc.; *top* Guy Jarvis/School Division/Houghton Mifflin Co.; **23** *grapes* PhotoObjects/Jupiterimages Corp.; *the rest* Guy Jarvis/School Division/Houghton Mifflin Co.; **24** *whole pineapple* Jim Jurica/ShutterStock; *halved pineapple* Rudolf Georg/ShutterStock; *the rest* Guy Jarvis/School Division/Houghton Mifflin Co.; **28** *left* Ed Kashi/Corbis; *right* HIRB/Index Stock Imagery; **29** *teen girl,* both Edward Hernandez/Edward H. Photos; *gift* PhotoDisc; **33** Antonio Colinas Victor Lerena/Agencia EFE; *book* Guy Jarvis/School Division/Houghton Mifflin Co.; **34** *bottom* Yanik Chauvin/ ShutterStock; *book* Guy Jarvis/School Division/Houghton Mifflin Co.; **38** Ken Welsh/age fotostock; **39** *both* Yadid Levy/Alamy; **43** *bottom* Larry Luxner/DDB Stock Photography; *top left* McDougal Littell/Houghton Mifflin Co.; *background* Guy Jarvis/School Division/Houghton Mifflin Co.; *sky* Val Maun/McDougal Littell/Houghton Mifflin Co.; **44** *top* Gonzalo Azumendi/age fotostock; *background* Guy Jarvis/School Division/Houghton Mifflin Co.; **48** Michael Moody/DDB Stock Photography; **49** Danny Lehman/Corbis; **53** *top* Jessica L. Archibald/ShutterStock; *top upper center* Galina Barskaya/ ShutterStock; *center* Jorge Albán/McDougal Littell/Houghton Mifflin Co.; *bottom lower center* Paul Yates/ShutterStock; *bottom* Spencer Jones/Getty Images; **54** *karate* Royalty-Free/Corbis; *volleyball* Roy Morsch/age fotostock; *the rest* LWA-Stephen Welstead/Corbis; **58** *left* Jorge Silva/Reuters/Corbis; *right* Tim De Waele/Corbis; **59** *both* Reuters/Corbis; **63** *bottom* Dynamic Graphics/Photis/Alamy; **63, 64** *computer* Tan Kian Khoon/ShutterStock; **68** Beryl Goldberg; **69** Agencia EFE; **73** *left* Mitch Diamond/ Alamy; *top right* Kevin Schafer/Getty Images; *bottom right* Stuart Westmorland/Getty Images; *scrapbook* Guy Jarvis/School Division/Houghton Mifflin Co.; **74** *beach* Jerry Driendl/Getty Images; *shell* PhotoDisc; *scrapbook* Guy Jarvis/School Division/Houghton Mifflin Co.; *the rest* Jorge Albán/ McDougal Littell/Houghton Mifflin Co.; **78** Frank Pedrick/The Image Works; **79** *top* Sonda Dawes/The Image Works; *bottom* PhotoDisc. **123** Lee Foster/Bruce Coleman, Inc.; **133** Timothy Fadek/Corbis; **135** *quinceañera* Martha Granger/EDGE Productions; *Sweet 16 party* Ryan McVay; **137** Dennis MacDonald/ PhotoEdit; **139** © 1978 George Ballis/Take Stock; **143** Jacques Jangoux/Getty Images

All other photos by Lawrence Migdale/PIX/McDougal Littell/Houghton Mifflin Co.